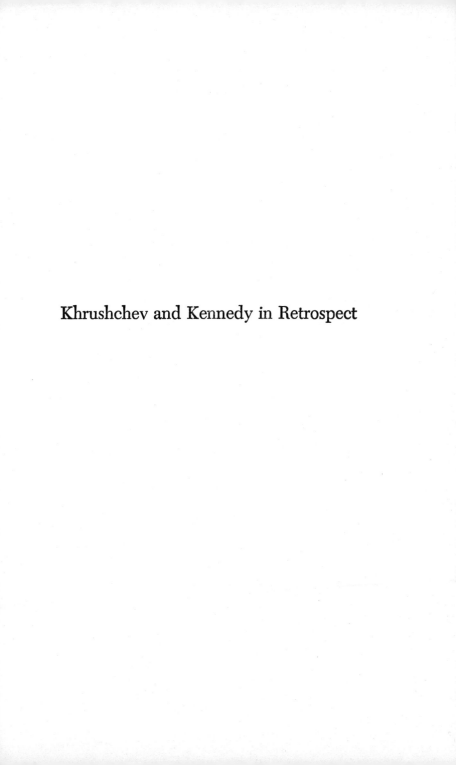

Khrushchev and Kennedy in Retrospect

by the same author:

Stalin, Hitler, and Europe: The Origins of World War II, 1933–1939
Stalin, Hitler and Europe: The Imbalance of Power, 1939–1941

KHRUSHCHEV

AND

KENNEDY

IN

RETROSPECT

JAMES E. McSHERRY

The Open-Door Press   PALO ALTO, CALIFORNIA

ISBN: 0–912162–01–5

LIBRARY OF CONGRESS CATALOG CARD: 70–123184

COPYRIGHT © 1971 BY JAMES E. MCSHERRY

Printed in the United States of America by
The George Banta Company

Preface

COMMUNIST leaders have repeatedly proclaimed the grand strategy and ultimate aims of Soviet policy, but Moscow shrouds its day-to-day tactics in an almost impenetrable and constantly renewed pall of propaganda—and not all necessarily false. The propaganda machine grinds out the official line, once established, in n languages and paraphrases; the line also varies according to the audience: After Khrushchev's speech to the Twentieth Party Congress in 1956, members of the Party apparatus and the more important members of Soviet society, senior army officers, factory managers, and government officials, could admit to one another their relief at Stalin's death and that he was really "Josef the Terrible." But to the rank and file of Soviet society he remained a Great Leader until the Twenty-Second Party Congress in 1961 and the reduction of the gruesome twosome in the mausoleum on Red Square once again to the singular.

For these reasons, serious historians seldom venture beyond the well-blazed trails of the revolution and civil war. Political "scientists" are somewhat braver, but their union rules forbid a straightforward account of what actually seems to have happened. And they usually examine single facets of Soviet policy: Cuba, China, Berlin, etc. Rather like the blind men and the elephant, no one considers the whole beast. Several journalists are capable of turning out an account better than any yet written, but since they *are* capable and always have deadlines to meet, they never have time to review, sift, and weigh any large mass of evidence.

Although the pertinent volumes of the *Foreign Relations of the United States* series can scarcely appear before twenty years, one may examine recent developments in Soviet-American relations with some confidence. Statements by officials of the U.S. Government and rumors and leaks in the American press are significant as the main source of information upon which Soviet policy-makers had to base their decisions. Several memoirs of the Kennedy administration confirm and supplement such press sources. Soviet newspapers are also useful if we ask ourselves not whether a given item was true or false but rather what effect it was designed to produce abroad. Indeed, in times of stress and crisis, Soviet pronouncements, taken in context with the events, can be very revealing. And anyone who talked as much as Khrushchev was bound to let the cat out of the bag occasionally.

J. E. McS.

June 1970

Contents

Khrushchev and Kennedy in Retrospect

Introduction

AT FIRST GLANCE the term "absolute monarchy" seems incompatible with the term "constitution." Nevertheless, the absolute monarchies of eighteenth-century Europe possessed very real if limited constitutions. Two basic provisions existed: (1) unlike Charlemagne's empire and some medieval Russian principalities, the state remained intact upon the death of the ruler; (2) generally acknowledged rules secured the orderly succession of the new sovereign—"The King is dead, long live the King!" But in the eighteenth century as in the twentieth, Russia was the great exception. The tsar would choose his own successor, decreed Peter the Great in 1722—and died three years later without naming one. Although Paul I (1796–1801) repealed Peter's edict and provided for an orderly succession, he himself was murdered, and not until after 1825 did the accession of a new tsar invariably take place under peaceful circumstances.

Peter completed a social revolution, breaking the power of the old boyar nobility and installing new men from every class as civil servants and gentry. These new men received privileges but had to pay for them by service in the army and government administration. Palace intrigues and revolutions marked the hundred years following Peter's death, and tsars who offended the gentry and the guards regiments seldom survived very long. Thus, by the time of Catherine II (died

11

1796), although the gentry retained their privileges, the state no longer required their services.

Lenin and Stalin also carried out a social revolution, expropriating and in many cases extirpating civil servants, army officers, and members of the growing commercial, industrial, and professional middle class. They too failed to establish a generally recognized succession; indeed, they seem to have reduced Russia to a somewhat more primitive political condition than had Peter. Although it is difficult to physically divide a modern, industrialized state, Stalin's heirs did something very similar immediately after his death: They divided up the state power—the sudden decline in the number of ministries and the size of the Party Presidium reflected this division.

As in eighteenth-century Russia, palace intrigues and revolutions have characterized post-Stalin politics. The four most important events were the combination of practically all Stalin's other heirs against Beria in 1953, the Khrushchev-Zhukov alliance against the Party Presidium in June 1957, Khrushchev's *coup d'état* which ousted Zhukov in the autumn of that year, and the fall of Khrushchev himself in October 1964.

As the eighteenth-century successors of Peter the Great appeased the new gentry, so Nikita Sergeyevich Khrushchev appeased not only the new Soviet middle class but Soviet society as a whole. Before his death in 1953, Stalin enjoyed the blind loyalty of most of the younger generation, inspired visceral fear in their elders, and ordered the U.S.S.R.'s foreign and domestic policies with little regard for Soviet public opinion. Khrushchev, on the other hand, never achieved this unquestioned if fearful acceptance and had to pursue policies calculated to enhance his personal popularity and prestige. He was never strong enough to use the "stick" and depended on "carrot" tactics. Thus he demanded more meat and better quarters for Soviet citizens and in his diplomacy posed as the great champion of peace and coexistence. This latter pose was particularly important in view of the Soviet peoples' bitter experiences in World War II and their fear of another war.

But a new factor has appeared on the scene since the eighteenth century: Modern propaganda techniques, exploiting press, radio, cinema, and television, make it comparatively easy for a ruler to achieve general popular acceptance. After a few years in control of the propaganda apparatus he can consider himself reasonably safe from a coup. In 1933, for example, any Reichswehr general could have ordered Hitler's arrest; a few years later, however, soldiers and junior officers would have refused to obey such an order. Even in 1944, when Hitler had clearly led Germany to the brink of disaster, the generals had no choice but to assassinate him. And when the major commanding the Berlin garrison battalion learned that the Führer was still alive, he promptly arrested the conspirators.

In 1957 Khrushchev's crudity, seeming impulsiveness and bumbling good nature, and general lack of dignity tended to offend the average Russian. Significantly, of his three major opponents, Molotov, Malenkov, and Kaganovich, only Molotov was exiled (1957–61) beyond the borders of the Soviet Union, first to Outer Mongolia and then to Vienna. Molotov hardly posed a threat in his own right. According to an apocryphal story long current in Moscow, Lenin once termed him the "best file clerk in Russia." As Chairman of the Council of

People's Commissars (1930–41) and in other capacities while Stalin lived, he scarcely dared sneeze on his own initiative. Nevertheless, he was one of the few surviving Old Bolsheviks (pre 1917), practically the only one closely associated with Lenin himself, and was widely respected by the Soviet public. In other words he would have been the perfect front-man for an anti-Khrushchev conspiracy.

By the end of 1961, however, Khrushchev's widely advertised championship of popular policies had won him general acceptance with the great majority of Soviet citizens. His numerous trips abroad, which Soviet communications media could publicize without an obvious propaganda build-up, were invaluable in establishing the image, at home at least, of an indefatigable seeker after peace. In overthrowing him in October 1964, Khrushchev's opponents probably acted at the eleventh hour. Given another year or so of control over the propaganda machine, he would have been practically invulnerable. Indeed, the anti-Khrushchev cabal considered his prestige too great to permit a simple announcement that he had been kicked out. Instead he was allegedly relieved at his own request because of age and ill health. In contrast Molotov, Malenkov, and Kaganovich, as well as Zhukov, were publicly attacked by name a few days after they had been ousted.

Even in October 1964 the conspirators might not have acted without a lucky conjuncture of circumstances. The Soviet Premier had left the capital September 30 for a vacation at Sochi on the Black Sea, and Anastas I. Mikoyan, who had helped foil a move to depose Khrushchev in 1957, was with him as late as October 12.

Another important factor was the absence of Mikhail A.

Kharlamov, chief of Soviet radio and television. (The editors of *Izvestia* and *Pravda* may also have been away from Moscow.) Had Kharlamov been in Moscow at any time before the (rump?) Central Committee convened, reportedly during the evening of October 13, he might conceivably have frustrated the coup with several television and radio announcements to the effect that "a conspiracy against the Soviet Government and Communist Party and against Comrade N. S. Khrushchev" had been uncovered, and that "detachments of the Soviet Army" had been alerted to take any action deemed necessary. Had a vote been taken immediately after such a demonstration that the Premier still held the reins of power, the conspirators could scarcely have held an anti-Khrushchev majority together. Indeed, the members of the Central Committee might have given Nikita Sergeyevich a unanimous vote of confidence—to demonstrate their loyalty and save their own skins.

With Kharlamov absent, however, the conspirators could have made their own announcement, had one been necessary: that Khrushchev had been dismissed. With news of a *fait accompli* and apparent proof of the coup's success ringing in their ears, few members of the Central Committee would have been brave enough to support a person who already seemed powerless.

In a dispatch from Moscow on October 24, 1964, Henry Tanner of the *New York Times* referred to "the microphone, which is as good a symbol of power as anything in this country." But it is more than a symbol—almost the essence.

1

Zhukov and the Syrian "Crisis"
(June–November 1957)

KHRUSHCHEV'S moves in the fall of 1957 furnish the clearest example of the importance he attached to maintaining a reputation as a man of peace and, conversely, of labeling his opponents as "warmongers." At that time, as the First Secretary of the Communist Party, he blew up a war scare and under its cover ousted his most dangerous rival, Marshal Georgi K. Zhukov. The marshal apparently never considered himself as such, and it would probably be too much to call him the ultimate ruler of the Soviet Union at the beginning of October 1957. But Nikita Sergeyevich quite clearly regarded him as a very powerful figure during the preceding three months.

The First Secretary's position as the most collected of the collective leadership had declined sharply following the revolt in Hungary and the near uprising in Poland in the fall of 1956. Rumor had him almost ousted as Party leader at a December 1956 meeting of the Central Committee. Although Khrushchev appeared to have regained most of his former authority by the spring of 1957, upon returning in mid-June from a visit to Finland he was confronted with a revolt in the Party Presidium led by Molotov, Malenkov, and Kaganovich.

"We are seven to your four," they said, "resign!"

"Seven to four may be a majority in arithmetic," replied Nikita Sergeyevich, "but not necessarily in politics"[1]—and he added Zhukov to his column and was thus able to move the dispute to the larger Central Committee where the marshal's support proved decisive. (The anti-Khrushchev majority may have evaporated, together with the courage of several Presidium members, even before the Central Committee met.)

According to the account Louis Fischer heard in Poland,[2] Zhukov produced from the security-police files a letter to Stalin. In 1936 Leo Kamenev, one of the early Bolshevik leaders, had written from prison in his own blood that he was being tortured; on the margin Molotov had ordered, "More torture." While this story may be true, the decisive factor was not Molotov's implication in Stalin's purge (Khrushchev and many other Central Committee members also had blood on their hands) but rather that the man who spoke for the Soviet armed forces was backing the Party First Secretary. The members of the Central Committee and all of the Soviet upper and middle classes, the senior bureaucrats, Party officials, military officers, and factory managers, had dreadful memories of the Great Purge of the thirties and Stalin's postwar terror. Although surviving physically, most of them were broken morally. Any convictions and personal loyalties they may have had were a poor second to the fear of being on the losing side in an internal political struggle. Had Marshal Zhukov resolutely marched a rifle company into the Kremlin at the beginning of October and arrested Khrushchev (who held no official position) and his followers on the first charge he could think of, most of the Soviet middle and upper classes would have climbed on the marshal's band wagon with alacrity.

In addition to authority over the politically decisive segment of Soviet society, Zhukov possessed a large measure of popularity with the Soviet public. He represented an institution, the army, which enjoyed far more popular respect than the Party. Alone among the leaders he could not be linked to Stalin's purges but had in fact been banished from Moscow after the war as a result of his personal prestige as the conqueror of Berlin. His popularity was demonstrated during a naval review at Leningrad on July 14, 1957. According to Max Frankel of the *New York Times,* "The crowd waved and roared cheers" as the marshal was ferried to the reviewing station, an anchored cruiser. The launch that returned him to shore passed within fifty yards of the crowded bank of the Neva: "The crowd went wild. Hundreds of men and women, many with children on their shoulders, pushed through the throng, running and stumbling after the vessel for a second and third look at the beaming military hero."[3]

From the end of June, Khrushchev apparently felt that he held his post only on Zhukov's sufferance. On September 22 the Yugoslav Government announced a pending visit by the marshal. During Zhukov's absence the First Secretary could engineer his dismissal as Defense Minister and thus eliminate the possibility of a military coup. Such a move, however, would neither destroy the marshal's personal popularity nor remove him from the Party Presidium. In Khrushchev's opinion something more was necessary: Zhukov must be branded as a "warmonger."

18

In addition to Stalin's terror, one other experience was engraved in the memories of all adult Soviet citizens, the suffering endured during World War II. Following a 4,000-mile tour oɪ the U.S.S.R., William J. Jorden of the *New York Times* on June 28, 1957 reported one of his strongest impressions, the "intense and sincere hope . . . that there should be no war. The thought that there might be and the fear of the consequences if there should be seem uppermost in the minds of the vast majority of simple people." "Not a few, for example, felt that during the Korean War and the recent revolt in Hungary a general war was imminent." Most Russians whom he met, noted another American who traveled widely in the U.S.S.R. during the summer of the same year, "insisted that Khrushchev was really for peace and for improved relations with the West." "Again and again these people emphasized their horror of another war."[4]

Khrushchev had played upon this general fear of war before. The June 29, 1957 resolution of the Central Committee expelling the "anti-Party group" stressed Molotov's opposition to steps to relieve tension: "The group attempted in effect to oppose the Leninist policy of peaceful coexistence between states with different social systems, of relaxing international tension and establishing friendly relations between the U.S.S.R. and all the people of the world." "For a long time, Comrade Molotov, in his capacity as foreign minister [until 1956] . . . repeatedly came out against the measures which the Presidium . . . was carrying out to improve relations with Yugoslavia." "Comrade Molotov raised obstacles to the conclusion of the state treaty with Austria" and "was also against normalization of relations with Japan . . . He opposed the fundamental proposition worked out by the party on the possibility of preventing wars in the present conditions . . . Comrade Molotov repeatedly opposed the Soviet Government's indispensable new steps in defense of peace and the security of nations."[5]

Developments in the Middle East afforded Khrushchev the opportunity he needed. At the end of April 1957 an unsuccessful attempt was made to overthrow King Hussein of Jordan. After a general strike and ineffective riots, the King imposed martial law and formed a new government. Washington ordered the Sixth Fleet from the Western to the Eastern Mediterranean, and Turkey concentrated troops on the Syrian frontier. Some vituperative propaganda statements about the movement of the Sixth Fleet, the Eisenhower Doctrine, and U.S. designs on the Middle East constituted the only Soviet reaction. Although the Syrian Government protested the Turkish troop concentrations, Moscow avoided the subject in its pronouncements.

Earlier shipments of Soviet arms to Syria had aroused fears in the West that the country was coming under Moscow's influence. On August 13, 1957 the Syrian Government expelled the military attaché and two other members of the U.S. Embassy staff. On the 15th it was announced that the Chief of Staff of the Syrian Army had resigned, and two days later General Afif Bizri, generally regarded as a Communist sympathizer, succeeded him. Observers in Turkey and the West feared Syria was sliding rapidly toward the left. Thinking perhaps to furnish any moderates in the Syrian Government with good arguments, Ankara ordered more troops to the frontier.

Turkey "might find herself at the bottom of a precipice," warned Soviet Foreign Minister Gromyko on September 10.[6]

There was much more danger than in the past, he declared, of local wars turning into a world war. The following day, however, the Soviet Ambassador to Ankara gave Turkish Premier Menderes a personal letter from Soviet Premier Bulganin. The tone of the letter was quite mild; Moscow seemed to be trying to reassure rather than threaten Turkey.[7]

In the evening of October 4, Zhukov left Moscow for the Crimea where he boarded a Soviet cruiser and sailed for Yugoslavia. Khrushchev was vacationing at Yalta. He immediately hurried back to the capital and on the afternoon of October 7 granted an interview to James Reston of the *New York Times*. During the conversation the First Secretary could hardly wait to discuss Turkey. He declared that Ankara, instigated by "American ruling circles," was still moving troops to the Syrian frontier. His subsequent remarks were much stronger than Bulganin's letter of September 11: "We cannot remain passive," he warned, "Turkey is our neighbor and has a long common frontier with us. We would like to caution the Turkish Government against rash adventurist steps which can push it into the abyss of war out of which Turkey will find it difficult to escape." "Turkey is concentrating her forces at the Syrian frontier. She is even laying bare certain parts of her frontier with the Soviet Union. But she should certainly not be doing this." "The U.S.A. after all is a long way away from this region, whereas we are neighbor on it."

On October 12 an official of the Soviet Embassy in London delivered a letter from Khrushchev to Hugh Gaitskell, the leader of the British Labour Party. The Socialist parties of the Netherlands, Denmark, Norway, France, Italy and Belgium received similar letters at about the same time. The

First Secretary appealed for Western Socialist support in preventing aggression by Turkey. In the letter to London he warned that "widening of the conflict around Syria may drive Britain into the abyss of a new destructive war with all its terrible consequences for the population of the British Isles."[8]

Turkish troops had attempted two raids on Syria within the last week, declared the Moscow radio on October 14, and Turkish planes had flown over the border. Two days later Soviet Foreign Minister Gromyko charged that Turkey had concentrated 500 tanks and 50,000 men on her southern border and intended to attack Syria after the Turkish elections scheduled for October 27. If the attack were actually carried out, "the member states of the United Nations should immediately render Syria the armed assistance necessary to put a stop to aggression. The Soviet government . . . is prepared to take part with its forces in suppressing aggression and punishing the violators of peace."[9] Moscow radio broadcast the text of the charge the following evening, and a *New York Times* correspondent reported that "the extensive propaganda campaign of Soviet news media to emphasize the Middle East situation has had an effect on a considerable number of Soviet citizens. The tendency of many people here is to regard the situation with increasing concern."

On the 18th a TASS release repeated the charge that the United States was inciting Turkey to attack Syria. "Nobody should entertain any doubts," it concluded, "that in the event of an attack on Syria, the U.S.S.R.—guided by the aims and principles of the United Nations Charter and by the interests of its own security—will take all necessary measures in order to extend assistance to the victim of aggression."[10]

"Alarmed stories about the danger of war in the Middle

East dominated the Soviet press today," reported Max Frankel on October 20, "The combined effect of this capital's newspapers tended to recreate the atmosphere that gripped Moscow almost exactly a year ago during the Hungarian and Suez crises." The following day a Soviet Foreign Ministry spokesman refused to deny reports that Soviet troops were massing on the Turkish frontier.

In an address to the United Nations General Assembly on the 22nd, Gromyko made the strongest official Soviet statement during the crisis: "The Soviet Union being guided by the purposes and principles of the United Nations charter and the interests of its security would, in the event of such an attack on Syria, take all the necessary steps to extend assistance to the victim of aggression."[11] The next day it was announced in Tiflis that Marshal Konstantin Rokossovsky, one of the outstanding Soviet field commanders of World War II, had assumed command of the Transcaucasian military district adjacent to Turkey.

Sometime before the 25th, the Presidium of the Supreme Soviet, the highest governmental body in the U.S.S.R., convened and officially relieved Zhukov as Defense Minister and appointed Marshal Malinovsky in his stead. According to one report the units of the Moscow military district were assembled for political briefings on the 25th and informed of the change. No public announcement was made at the time, however. If the reported briefings actually took place, it meant that Zhukov could no longer carry out a *coup d'état* after the 25th, i.e. he could no longer simply take charge of the nearest body of troops in his capacity as Defense Minister and arrest the nongovernmental members of the Party Presidium.

Zhukov had arrived in Belgrade on October 8 and proceeded to Tiranë on the 17th. He flew back from Albania on October 26 and was met at the Moscow airport by a delegation which included his successor, Marshal Malinovsky, the chiefs of the navy and air force, the commander of the Moscow military district, and Marshal Konev. The delegation's mission was evidently to convince Zhukov that he would find no support among the senior officers of the armed forces. At 7:30 that evening the Soviet public heard the brief announcement of the marshal's relief over the radio.

Zhukov no longer had an official government post; it only remained to remove him from the Party Presidium. The Central Committee met "late in October" according to the official announcement, probably on or after the 28th. As things turned out the war scare was hardly necessary. The First Secretary evidently had no need to fear the marshal's personal popularity, in the Central Committee at least. His own band wagon was forging triumphantly ahead while that of the now powerless Zhukov was obviously falling apart. The average Central Committee member had little difficulty in deciding which one to board. "Socialist realism" (in a nonliterary and meaningful sense) won out in only three or four days; in contrast the ouster of Malenkov, Molotov, *et al.* four months earlier had required a week of debate.

The matter may have been decided by October 29. That morning at the United Nations, Gromyko adopted a relatively mild tone; he declared that the United States was "playing with fire" but failed to repeat his earlier warning of Soviet support for Syria. The same evening Khrushchev, Bulganin, and Mikoyan attended a Turkish Embassy reception. The First Secretary, in an ebullient mood, proclaimed his presence a "gesture, a gesture toward peace." When questioned about Zhukov's fate (no new announcement had been made), Khrushchev declared, "You can sleep calmly tonight, tomorrow night and on the nights after; sleep is a good thing."[12] According to an Associated Press correspondent in Moscow, he also damned "him who thinks of war! Let him be damned who wants war! He who wants war, let him fight alone." If the U.S.S.R. could decide the matter, he added, "there would be no war for hundreds of centuries."

In the two or three days following the plenary meeting of the Central Committee, Party officials explained the ouster at local Party meetings. The text of the resolution expelling Zhukov from the Central Committee and Presidium was not released until November 2.[13] The former Defense Minister, the resolution emphasized, had "pursued a policy of curtailing the work of party organizations . . . of abolishing the leadership and control of the Party." The text also charged that "the cult of Comrade Zhukov's personality was cultivated in the Soviet Army with his personal participation"; that "he was praised to the sky" and "his person and role in the Great Patriotic War were over-glorified."

In local Party discussions, however, the Party leaders probably stressed the charge that "he proved to be a politically unsound person, inclining to adventurism, both in his understanding of the prime objective of the Soviet Union's foreign policy and in his leadership of the Ministry of Defense." In other words he was a "warmonger." (Questioned by reporters at a diplomatic reception on June 9, 1959, Defense Minister Malinovsky said that Zhukov was drawing his pension and writing his memoirs and had "learned to fish quite well.")[14]

The liquidation of the "crisis," started on October 29, continued. In a press statement issued at the United Nations on November 2, Gromyko declared a threat to Syria still existed but spoke of the "crisis" generally in the past tense. The next day a Soviet periodical printed statements made by Khrushchev to a Canadian journalist: The First Secretary saw no "danger of war in the near future" since "we do not have an eve-of-war situation like that, for example, prior to the Second World War."[15] And on the 5th *Izvestia* published an Iranian letter of three weeks earlier in which the Shah expressed confidence that Turkey had no intention of attacking any of her neighbors.

In a speech to the Supreme Soviet on November 6, Khrushchev closed on a very soft line: Although "ideological differences" between capitalism and communism were "irreconcilable," they did not preclude "peaceful coexistence, peaceful competition between Socialist and capitalist countries." "Though we are convinced that if a new war were unleashed . . . the Socialist system would win, we Communists do not aspire for victory in this way. . . . for the victory of socialism wars are not needed."[16]

By the end of 1957 Khrushchev seemed to be the undisputed leader in the U.S.S.R. He had apparently reached the point Stalin had reached in 1930. Unlike Stalin, however, who waited until 1941 to assume the post of Premier or Chairman of the Council of Ministers (then People's Commissars), the First Secretary took over this position on March 27, 1958, only five months after he overcame Zhukov. In the future, should a "politically unsound person, inclining to adventurism" ever be in a position to give such an order, troops who might not hesitate to seize the leader of the Communist Party could be expected to think twice before attempting to arrest the head of the Soviet Government.

2

From Beirut to Berlin—
via Quemoy
(July–November 1958)

ENCOURAGED by the success of the October coup, the absence of any adverse reaction from the Soviet Army, and his personal control over both Party and government, Khrushchev evidently considered the situation at home safe enough for him to adopt a harder attitude abroad. Relations with Yugoslavia deteriorated immediately after he became Chairman of the Council of Ministers. Earlier he had repeatedly urged a summit conference, but now seemed comparatively indifferent to the idea. And on June 17, 1958 "Hungarian" authorities announced the execution of Imre Nagy, premier at the time of the uprising, General Pal Maleter, and two other Hungarians.

At 3:00 A.M. on July 14, 1958, army officers overthrew an authoritarian but responsible and pro-Western government in Iraq. The Suez crisis had seriously weakened the Western position in the Middle East, disorders already troubled Lebanon, and now the whole area seemed about to dissolve in political chaos. Looking southward from the Kremlin,

Communist prospects must have seemed very bright indeed.

But at 9:20 A.M. on the 15th the White House announced that Marines had been dispatched to Lebanon at the request of the Lebanese Government, and at 3:00 that afternoon, local time, the first boatload touched the beach at Beirut. Before the day was out, a Soviet representative had introduced a resolution at the United Nations calling on the United States "to remove its troops from the territory of Lebanon immediately."[1] That evening TASS called the landing an "open act of aggression." The next day Soviet authorities in Moscow handed U.S. Ambassador Thompson a formal protest. The Soviet Union, it warned, "cannot remain indifferent to events creating a grave menace in an area adjacent to its frontiers and reserves the right to take the necessary measures dictated by the interests of peace and security."[2]

The following day, July 17, British paratroops landed in Jordan at the invitation of King Hussein's government, and on the 18th the British and American ambassadors received an official statement from the Soviet Foreign Ministry. But the statement merely repeated the earlier "warning," that "the Soviet Union will not rest indifferent to the acts of unprovoked aggression" and would be "compelled to take the necessary steps dictated by the interests of the Soviet Union's security and the safeguarding of world peace."[3]

These were obviously statements for the record. The vigorous U.S. reaction to the revolt in Iraq may or may not have caused anxiety in the Kremlin, but in their actions Soviet authorities displayed a noticably milder attitude. East German and American Red Cross representatives signed an agreement in East Berlin on July 17 providing for the release of eight U.S. Army officers and a sergeant whose helicopter had landed in East Germany by mistake on June 7. The East-zone regime had previously sought governmental negotiations, i.e. *de facto* recognition. The men were released on the 19th, and in a message to President Eisenhower the same day Khrushchev proposed a summit conference of the "heads of Government of the U.S.S.R., the U.S.A., Britain, France and India, with the participation of the Secretary General of the U.N." The conference would "work out concrete recommendations for the cessation of the military conflict" in the Middle East, and the Soviet Premier proposed "to meet on any day and at any time, and the sooner the better." Khrushchev suggested a meeting at Geneva on July 22, but said any other place, even Washington, was agreeable. "We are addressing you not from an attitude of intimidation," he wrote, "but from an attitude of reason."[4] On July 22 at a Polish Embassy reception, the Soviet Premier spent an hour and a half with Ambassador and Mrs. Thompson. The ambassador told reporters no important political matters were discussed but he interpreted the conversation as a friendly gesture.

The Western powers replied on the 22nd. President de Gaulle seemed lukewarm to the idea, but Prime Minister Macmillan urged a meeting at the Security Council. Under the United Nations Charter, pointed out President Eisenhower, heads of government could represent their countries at Security Council meetings. "If such a meeting were generally desired, the United States would join in following that orderly procedure."[5]

The first Soviet reaction was negative. "One may well ask what kind of simpleton do the American leaders calculate on?" asked "Observer" in *Izvestia* on the 23rd. "Everybody knows the United States possesses a mechanical majority in the Security Council. Moreover, does the United States really think that anyone would consent to discuss major international problems with Chiang Kai-shek, who, by the grace of his American patrons, occupies a seat in the Security Council?" But in a message to Eisenhower later in the day, Khrushchev seized on the idea and urged that Nehru and Hammarskjold attend and the Arab governments participate. He suggested a meeting in New York on July 28.[6]

In a letter to the Soviet Premier two days later, President Eisenhower recommended preliminary arrangements by the permanent representatives on the Security Council after they had determined that such a meeting was generally acceptable. And July 28 "would be too early for us."[7] The same day (25th) a Western source at the United Nations headquarters predicted a Security Council meeting within a week or ten days to arrange a summit conference.

An article in *Pravda* on July 27 accused the United States of "unscrupulous dodges and maneuvers" to delay a summit meeting. President Eisenhower had not even mentioned an approximate date, and Washington sought to "drown a conference in a sea of red tape." And in a letter to Eisenhower the next day, Khrushchev charged the U.S. Government with "delaying the convocation of a conference," with "trying in every way to hinder the solution of the main question of the moment, . . . the ending of the armed Anglo-United States intervention in the Middle East. It is seeking to drag the negotiations on a meeting of heads of governments into a labyrinth of endless discussions about the form and procedure of that meeting." Nevertheless, the Soviet Premier again urged a summit as soon as possible. Since July 28 was too early for the United States, "we are ready for another early date and

would like to receive a clear answer when the U.S.A. is prepared to take part . . . I would like the earliest reply to this
message, Mr. President."[8]

But three days later, on July 31, Khrushchev was conferring with Mao Tse-tung and other Chinese leaders in Peking.
In addition to the Premier, Defense Minister Malinovsky,
Deputy Foreign Minister Vasily V. Kuznetsov (Soviet Ambassador to China in 1953), and Boris N. Ponomarev, a Central Committee member concerned with relations with other
Communist parties, represented the U.S.S.R. According to
the official communiqué, the Chinese present included Premier Chou En-lai, Defense Minister Marshal Peng Teh-huai,
Foreign Minister Chen Yi, and a member of the Chinese
Central Committee Secretariat, Wang Chia-hsiang, a special-
ist on inter-party relations.[9]

We can only speculate on the discussions. In view of who
went where, however, one might conclude that Khrushchev
wanted something from Mao and not the reverse. Did the
Soviet Premier admit his sore straits and ask for help? Did he
ask for a demonstration against the Nationalist-held offshore
islands which might deter further large-scale intervention by
U.S. forces in the Middle East? Or did he say something like
this: "Look, Comrade Mao! Now is your chance. The Americans are tied down in the Middle East, and you may count
on us for support if they do try to defend the islands." If he
used the latter gambit, it could explain, in part, the subsequent deterioration in Soviet-Chinese relations. (During the
1963 Sino-Soviet name calling and bean spilling, both parties
maintained a rather suspicious reticence about the events of
1958.)

During Khrushchev's absence from Moscow, Britain and

the United States had indicated—on July 31 and August 1—approval of an August 12 meeting. But reports from Washington on August 2 spoke of a conference on the 15th. In Washington on July 22, the Defense Department had given the strength of U.S. forces in Lebanon: 8,000 combat and 300 support troops. Reports from Beirut two days later spoke of some 4,000 soldiers and over 6,000 Marines. A transport with 1,800 Army troops, two engineer battalions and medical units, docked late in the evening of August 1. On the 3rd, 2,200 Army troops landed, and the total force was estimated at 13,300; 72 medium tanks were to be unloaded the next day.

Khrushchev arrived back in Moscow during the night of August 3 and on the 5th, in messages to Eisenhower, Macmillan, and de Gaulle, rejected the summit conference. The Security Council he wrote, "is virtually paralyzed and not in a state to adopt any decision independently of the United States." Since the U.S. and British governments "have made impossible the convocation of a conference of five powers," and the Security Council was powerless, the Soviet Government demanded "an extraordinary session of the United Nations General Assembly to discuss the question of the withdrawal of United States troops from Lebanon and British troops from Jordan"[10]

At the same time the Soviet Premier attempted to blame the Chinese for his abrupt about-face: "Without the Chinese People's Republic the Security Council and the United Nations cannot be a completely effective organ in the matter of preserving peace," he declared in his messages of the 5th. And Moscow judiciously leaked "inside" information to Polish Communists. From Warsaw on August 6, A. M. Rosenthal of the *New York Times* reported information from Polish sources: Mao had clearly indicated displeasure at Khrushchev's agreement to a Security Council meeting which would include a representative of Nationalist China. "The belief here is that Mr. Khrushchev had not expected to encounter such vehement opposition from Mr. Mao." "Polish Communist opinion," reported Mr. Rosenthal on the 17th, "still is that the Peiping meeting was a major factor behind Premier Khrushchev's decision to avoid a United Nations Security Council summit meeting. Communists here believe Mr. Mao made it clear he was against the idea of Mr. Khrushchev's sitting down at a council table with a representative of Nationalist China."

And a similar report came from Moscow on August 6. Roy Essoyan, a member of the Associated Press bureau, attempted to transmit a comparatively short dispatch. After it had been held by the censor for eight hours, Mr. Essoyan grew impatient and sent the story without clearance.[11] Presumably he expected no adverse reaction from higher Soviet authorities. "Peiping," he wrote, "is believed to have objected to a summit meeting at which its sworn enemy, Generalissimo Chiang Kai-shek, or one of his representatives would participate. . . . Mr. Mao is not alone. The line he advocates apparently has substantial support in the inner councils of the Kremlin. Mr. Khrushchev is no dictator. . . . Kremlin policies still seem to depend on the balance of majority opinion within its highest councils."

Many readers will recognize the last part of this tune. The words used to be "Poor Uncle Joe, the Prisoner of the Politburo." But in August 1958 the song may have had some validity. As we now know, several persons who were then members of the Party Presidium had sided with the "anti-

Party group" a year earlier. After U.S. forces landed in Lebanon, Nikita Sergeyevich apparently feared a similar occupation of Iraq and suppression of the revolution in that country, i.e. the extinction of the bright prospects for communism and the permanent return of strong Western forces to the Middle East. His enemies at home could have represented such a development as a reverse for the Soviet Union and thus weakened Khrushchev's personal position. Something similar had happened after the Suez and Hungarian crises of 1956.

Although Western authors of scholarly books and articles have repeatedly attributed the rejection of a summit to Chinese pressure, the first stanza seems to have been completely out of tune with the truth. As early as July 25 the *Jenmin Jih Pao* (People's Daily), the organ of the Chinese Party's Central Committee, had termed the Soviet Premier's proposal for a Security Council conference a "major step for peace." And if Britain and the United States continued to "stall" a five-power conference, Chou En-lai told a Cambodian economic mission in Peking at the end of the month, it would prove they were "deliberately bent on dragging the West, Asia and the whole world into a grave war catastrophe."[12] Even the joint Chinese-Soviet communiqué released at the end of Khrushchev's visit did not rule out a summit conference under United Nations auspices: "A conference of the heads of government of the big powers should be called at once to discuss the situation in the Near and Middle East," and Britain and the United States should "withdraw their forces immediately from Lebanon and Jordan."[13]

While attempting to evade responsibility for rejecting a summit conference, the Soviet Premier also sought to play down the danger in the Middle East and emphasize the possibility of an approaching crisis in the Far East. On the night of August 4, a day after his return from Peking, TASS published a statement Khrushchev had made to a group of Indian journalists in Moscow on July 29: He opposed volunteers, i.e. Soviet "volunteers," for the Middle East. As early as August 6, A. M. Rosenthal reported that the information reaching Warsaw indicated increased Soviet delivery of more modern weapons to Communist China. A similar report came from Moscow two days later. And on the 10th the London *Sunday Times* published a dispatch from Tokyo to the effect that Moscow had supplied China with a stock of atom bombs.

From Warsaw on the 17th, Mr. Rosenthal reported similar information: "The Soviet Union has decided to supply Communist China with atomic weapons and ballistic missiles." "It seems likely," he added, "that reports of Russian-sponsored modernization of China's military potential . . . are being allowed to circulate with at least the tacit approval of the Soviet Union. On Aug. 9 . . . a dispatch [to Warsaw?] was permitted to pass the Moscow censorship hinting the Soviet would help the Chinese in the military and atomic fields. It is not possible to determine on the basis of available information in Warsaw the full military implication of these reports or to what extent they are designed to impress the West." A very able and perceptive reporter, A. M. Rosenthal; indeed, a bit too perceptive for the taste of the Communist authorities who later expelled him from Poland.

During the last part of July, jet-equipped Chinese air units had occupied a number of bases near the southeast China coast, and on July 29 four MIG-17's shot down two of four Nationalist F-84's on a routine patrol near Swatow. On August 4 Communist batteries fired sixty-two rounds and on the 5th ninety rounds at Quemoy, Little Quemoy, and Tatan island. They fired thirty shells at Quemoy on the 6th, and Nationalist authorities declared an alert and ordered the evacuation of all noncombatant visitors from the offshore islands. Ten F-84's clashed with twelve MIG-17's over Quemoy on the 7th, but neither side suffered any losses. Before dawn on the 10th, Nationalist warships fired on four Communist ships near Matsu, and Communist artillery fired forty-one rounds on Quemoy during the night of August 10/11. Nationalist F-86's downed two MIG-17's southwest of Matsu on the 14th, and the Nationalist navy sank a Communist gunboat attempting to pick up the pilot of one of the planes. For their part, the Communists claimed the destruction of two F-86's off the Fukien coast and fired forty-four shells on Quemoy. The island received eighty-eight rounds during the first forty-five minutes of the 18th, and later in the day the Nationalist Defense Ministry reported eight or nine new Communist divisions on the mainland opposite Taiwan.

Finally, on August 23, 1958, the siege of Quemoy began. Between 6:30 and 8:30 P.M., local time, Communist batteries fired more than forty thousand shells on Quemoy and Little Quemoy. Although the defenders suffered two hundred military and a number of civilian casualties in this initial barrage, they were well emplaced and a bombardment posed no direct threat. But the Communist guns were within range of the landing beaches and for several weeks the Nationalist navy was unable to land any significant quantity of supplies.

In Washington during the morning of September 3, Secretary of State Dulles met with the chiefs of mission of the other S.E.A.T.O. powers. Late that afternoon he conferred with the Secretary and Deputy Secretary of Defense and the Chairman of the Joint Chiefs of Staff. According to "United States diplomatic sources," E. W. Kenworthy, a Washington correspondent of the *New York Times* reported the same day, "the United States would intervene if a Chinese communist attack on Quemoy threatened to overwhelm the Nationalists there." After conferring with President Eisenhower the next day at Newport, Rhode Island, Dulles issued a prepared statement. Referring to an earlier joint resolution of Congress on the defense of Taiwan, he stated that the President had not yet found a need for U.S. forces. But he would not "hesitate to make such a finding if he judged that the circumstances made this necessary." And in addition "the securing and protecting of Quemoy and Matsu have increasingly become related to the defense of Taiwan. . . . Military dispositions have been made by the United States so that a Presidential determination, if made, would be followed by action both timely and effective."[14]

The same day General Curtis Le May, the Air Force Vice Chief of Staff, took off for the Far East in a KC-135 jet accompanied by the Chinese Nationalist air attaché in Washington. And from the Philippines on the 4th, the Associated Press reported "probably the largest concentration of American air power in the Western Pacific since the Korean War."

These developments evidently impressed the Chinese Communist leaders. On September 6 the Peking radio broadcast in English the text of a statement by Premier Chou En-lai. Chou condemned Dulles' statement of the 4th, reaffirmed China's claim to Taiwan and the offshore islands, and said the U.S. measures would not cow the Chinese people. He declared (plaintively?) that "the United States, while not yet withdrawing its forces of aggression from Lebanon, has hastened to create a new danger of war in the Taiwan Strait area." Nevertheless, in "a further effort to safeguard peace, the Chinese Government is prepared to resume the ambassadorial talks [in Warsaw] between the two countries."[15] Communist batteries suspended the barrage the same day, and a Nationalist convoy was able to land supplies. After President Eisenhower had lunched with the Secretary of State and other members of the National Security Council, the White House on the 6th issued a statement taking "particular note" of the "reported radio statement of Mr. Chou En-lai . . . The United States Ambassador at Warsaw stands ready promptly to meet with the Chinese Communist Ambassador there, who has previously acted in this matter."[16]

Apparently Khrushchev felt he had to do something to encourage Peking and keep Washington worried about the situation in the Far East. Thus, during the evening of September 7 the U.S. chargé in Moscow received the text of a letter to Eisenhower. "An attack on the People's Republic of China," declared the Soviet Premier, "is an attack on the Soviet Union. We have a treaty of friendship, alliance and mutual assistance . . . a treaty meeting the fundamental interests of the Soviet and Chinese peoples . . . and may no one doubt that we shall completely honor our commitments."[17]

And on the 21st the Washington bureau of the *New York Times* ("Random Notes in Washington") reported the following: "For the last few weeks, Iron Curtain diplomats have been busy here emphasizing to anybody who will listen that Moscow really means it when it says Communist China will be fully backed in any war with the United States."

But the most amusing act (although hardly for the star) of this diplomatic drama was played out in Moscow on September 20 when the Foreign Ministry Press Department informed the chief of the Associated Press bureau that Roy Essoyan had committed "a rude violation of Soviet censorship" in connection with a dispatch transmitted early in August and must leave the U.S.S.R. within a week. In expelling Mr. Essoyan, Soviet officials were in effect denying the truth of his dispatch of August 6: Khrushchev had *not* rejected summit talks because of Chinese and "Stalinist" pressure and now supported Communist China, without reservation, of his own free will.[18] Nikita Sergeyevich may have been crude and *nekul'turnyy*, but one must admit to a certain sneaking respect for a person who, in this case at least, so deftly managed to eat his cake and have it too.

The Nationalist navy scored one of its first successes in supplying Quemoy on September 16 when an LST discharged its entire cargo, loaded amphibious craft, under fire within twenty minutes. (Hills on the island prevented observed fire by the mainland batteries.) The same day Quemoy received 6,840 shells between 6:00 A.M. and 9:00 P.M. The next day two ships landed supplies, but a Nationalist spokesman admitted that the techniques would have to be improved before the blockade could be considered broken. Two more LST's landed supplies on the 18th, and four Nationalist F-86's took on some sixteen MIG-17's—shooting down five of them without any losses of their own. Three ships landed supplies and withdrew without damage on the 19th, and on the 20th the Nationalists landed supplies for the seventh straight day. Although Taipei believed satisfactory landing techniques had been worked out, Hanson Baldwin pointed out that in a week six convoys had landed only enough supplies for about one day. And the Chinese Communists were probably firing less than half of their own shell production. "Thus the campaign of Quemoy is still undecided and neither side has engaged its full strength." Too, reports from Taipei on the 25th estimated the daily deliveries at not more than a sixth of normal requirements. But on the same day over a hundred MIG-17's attacked thirty-two Nationalist F-86's; Nationalist pilots shot down ten MIG's without any losses of their own. And on October 3 Hanson Baldwin, citing air superiority and improved landing techniques, declared the Nationalists were breaking the blockade. Nevertheless, he warned, the Communists could still change the picture by using greater strength and enlarging the theater of operations.

As early as August 8 a "responsible source" at Beirut had mentioned the pending withdrawal of a Marine battalion. Embarcation began on the 13th, but an "informed source" admitted the move was only a token withdrawal; the unit was to remain with the Sixth Fleet in the Mediterranean, and 9,000 Army troops and 3,000 Marines remained in Lebanon. According to an official announcement at Beirut on September 10, a second Marine battalion was to depart on September 15, leaving some 3,400 Marines and 7,000 to 8,000 soldiers in Lebanon. But the same day approximately 1,900 men of the 6th Marine Regiment began embarking at a North Carolina port for service with the Sixth Fleet.

On the 15th at Beirut, however, two battalions rather than one were loading aboard transports which sailed on the 16th. This left 8,015 Army troops and 1,600 Marines in Lebanon. The same day a complete withdrawal was unofficially predicted for about September 30, but in Washington on the

25th Administration sources mentioned the end of October. The last Marine battalion in Lebanon began loading its equipment on September 28 and sailed to join the Sixth Fleet on October 1. The same day King Hussein stated British troops would start withdrawing from Jordan on October 20.

But on October 3 it was revealed that a fresh Marine battalion had arrived from the United States on September 29. A Marine spokesman said the unit would stay in port a short time for liberty but would remain billeted aboard ship. Most of the Marines who left earlier may still have been in the Mediterranean and capable of again wading ashore at Beirut on a few hours' notice. On October 4, however, 1,000 Army troops loaded aboard a transport which sailed for Germany the next morning, and it was disclosed that the Air Force had flown out 730 soldiers in the preceding ten days.

This was the first indubitable withdrawal and may well have been the last straw of discouragement for Peking. Khrushchev and the Chinese Communists reacted almost simultaneously. In a statement given to TASS and released during the night of October 5, the Soviet Premier seized upon a remark by President Eisenhower at an October 1 news conference and denied that the Soviet Union would intervene in the Far East as long as the conflict remained between the two Chinese factions. And no shells fell on Quemoy after 1:00 A.M., local time, October 6; a large Nationalist supply convoy landed unopposed later in the morning. In a "message" to the Nationalists released the same day by the official mainland news agency, the Communist Defense Minister said he had ordered suspension of the shelling for one week and would allow supply operations. The Defense Minister extended the cease fire for two weeks on the 13th, but the bombardment began again on the 20th. This resumption, however, seems to have been nothing more than a "salute" for Secretary of State Dulles who arrived at Taipei on the morning of the 21st for talks with Chiang. No all-out effort at a siege followed, and on October 25 the Communists announced they would not fire on even dates.

In a speech on March 10, 1939, Stalin accused Britain and France of following the very policy he longed to be in a position to follow himself. Similarly, in the message to Eisenhower of September 7, 1958, Khrushchev may have accused the United States of following the very policy he hoped it *would* follow. He protested the U.S. role in the Quemoy crisis and sought to justify that of Communist China. The pertinent passages are as follows:

Warships and aircraft are being rushed to the Far East from the United States, the Mediterranean and other regions. . . . the practice of rushing United States warships from one place to another has in general become a frequent case of late. Indeed, it can be almost unmistakably determined where the next blackmail or provocation will occur by the movement of the American naval units. . . . The practice of dispatching naval fleets and air wings from one part of the world to another, for instance to the Middle East, the Far East . . . to bring pressure to bear now on some nations, now on others . . . It is a legitimate question to ask whether the United Nations should not consider this and take a decision forbidding the powers to undertake such movements of their naval and air forces for the purposes of blackmail and intimidation and obliging them to keep these forces within their national frontiers. . . . such dispatch of warships now in one direction, now in another . . .

Whatever the Soviet Premier's hopes, no significant increase in the strength of the U.S. forces in Lebanon occurred after the beginning of the Quemoy crisis; indeed, that crisis may have induced Washington to withdraw some of its forces earlier than planned. As seen from the Kremlin, the diversion in the Far East may well have paralyzed or at least seriously impeded American policy in the Middle East.

The political situation in that area remained extremely precarious. In Jordan King Hussein's position was by no means secure, civil disorders could again break out in Lebanon, and the new regime in Iraq gave no promise of stability. Communist prospects still appeared quite bright. Nevertheless, although the last U.S. troops left Beirut on October 25, Western intervention could again be expected in the event, e.g., of a Communist coup in Iraq. Should the Nationalists evacuate the offshore islands or Peking refuse to cooperate, it would be impossible to use the Quemoy maneuver a second time. Properly irritated, however, Berlin might prove an even more tender spot. A simple Western blockade of Iraq would soon spell the end of any Communist regime, but the Western powers could hardly take such a step if threatened with a blockade of Berlin. Hence, with a speech in Moscow on November 10, 1958, Khrushchev poured Berlin into the samovar where it has been simmering ever since.

The Western powers, he complained, "enjoy the right of unhampered communication between West Berlin and West Germany by air, rail, highways and the water of the G.D.R. [German Democratic Republic—East Germany] which they do not even wish to recognize." The Soviet Premier also accused the West of wholesale violation of the Potsdam Agreement, reviving German military might, etc.

The time has evidently come [he continued] for the powers which signed the Potsdam agreement to give up the remnants of the occupation regime in Berlin and thus make it possible to create a normal atmosphere in the capital of the G.D.R. The Soviet Union, for its part, will hand over those functions in Berlin which are still with Soviet organs to the sovereign German Democratic Republic. I think that this would be the right thing to do.

Let the United States, France and Britain form their own relations with G.D.R. and come to an agreement with it if they are interested in certain questions connected with Berlin. As for the Soviet Union, we shall observe as sacred our obligations which stem from the Warsaw treaty . . .

Should any aggressive forces attack the German Democratic Republic, which is an equal partner of the Warsaw Treaty, then we will consider it as an attack on the Soviet Union . . .[19]

After this speech the Soviet Premier carefully kept the Berlin crisis at the proper temperature (except perhaps for a few months in 1961), never allowing a real war scare to develop but never allowing the subject to drop from public attention. The Middle East remained surprisingly stable, but Berlin proved useful in other areas and ways, e.g., in extorting an invitation for Khrushchev to visit the United States in the fall of 1959 and Washington's agreement to a summit conference in 1960.

3

Powers and the Paris Fiasco
(May 1960)

WASHINGTON received Nikita Sergeyevich with some reserve but proper protocol in September 1959; the Soviet Premier toured the country and held cozy talks with President Eisenhower at Camp David. Well fueled by this event, the Soviet propaganda machine chugged happily along the tracks of peaceful coexistence, at home and abroad, for the next seven months. And after a number of diplomatic exchanges, the governments of Britain, France, the U.S.S.R., and the United States agreed to a summit conference in Paris during May 1960.

But on May 5, 1960 the Premier informed the Supreme Soviet that a U.S. plane flying over the territory of the U.S.S.R. on May 1 had been shot down. Two days later he disclosed that the U-2 plane had been flying across the Soviet Union on a photo-reconnaissance mission, had been downed in the heart of the U.S.S.R., and the pilot had been taken alive. That evening the State Department admitted the truth of Khrushchev's charge. In Paris on May 16, the scheduled opening day of the summit conference, the Soviet Premier effectively vetoed any negotiations by demanding as a prerequisite a public apology from President Eisenhower and punishment of those responsible for the U-2 incident.

Prestige plays a crucial role in the success of the Soviet system at home and abroad—prestige in the sense of fearful respect. Stalin enslaved the Czechs and Slovaks by intimidation in 1948, and Communist regimes currently hold over a hundred million of the peoples of Eastern Europe in subjugation mainly by the 1956 and 1968 demonstrations of Soviet power and ruthlessness in Hungary and Czechoslovakia.[1]

Before the first U-2 was shot down on May 1, a Soviet protest would have been a public confession of impotence. And Khrushchev could be reasonably sure the United States would not be the first to reveal the flights. After May 1, however, he naturally wished to prove the reconnaissance program no longer feasible. He could have made this point by quietly handing over the pilot to inform the C.I.A. that the plane had indeed been shot down. But, projecting his own attitudes upon others, the Soviet Premier probably thought Washington would interpret such a mild reaction as evidence of fear and weakness. And another danger existed: Aware that high-altitude flights were no longer practicable, Washington might decide to extract a final propaganda dividend. Soviet prestige would have suffered a terrible blow if, in the midst of some future campaign of Communist threats, the United States had published photos and announced that reconnaissance planes had been making regular flights across the U.S.S.R. The belated production in Moscow of a U-2 pilot and wreckage would have softened the blow only slightly. Thus, once the first plane was shot down, the Soviet

Government almost had to take the initiative in revealing the affair.

In remarks during the weeks following the incident, Khrushchev repeatedly betrayed concern over its prestige aspects. He made perhaps the most revealing statement at a Czechoslovak Embassy reception in Moscow on May 9. After the signing of an East German-Soviet peace treaty, said the Soviet Premier, should the Western powers attempt to force their way into West Berlin, "our force will resist this force."

Aware of this, some leaders in the United States of America decided to teach Khrushchev a lesson: Since it is said that force will resist force, we shall teach a lesson to the Soviet Union, we shall fly over your territory and we already flew over it and returned home. . . . the aggressive military wanted to demonstrate their strength once again fifteen days before the summit meeting.

Well, Khrushchev, what are you boasting of? We fly over your country and you can do nothing about it. They expected to fly over Soviet territory this time, too, to fly over Sverdlovsk and to show that we can do nothing about it. Indeed, an unpleasant situation.[2]

The Soviet Premier spoke with reporters at an exhibition of the U-2 wreckage in Moscow on May 11. "An unheard of action," he exclaimed. "And after all this I am expected to say: 'What nice people you are.' That would mean lacking in self-respect." Similarly—"what would you think of your government," he asked journalists in Paris on May 18, "if it treated with indifference, with unconcern, the overflights of your cities by military planes of countries of which you yourselves sometimes write as potential opponents? Would you respect such a government?"[3]

At the time many experts suspected the U-2 had been shot down by fighters after an engine failure and descent to a lower altitude. The sensitivity of Soviet propaganda to such suggestions also reflected concern over prestige. Upon returning from the trial in Moscow, the pilot's father told reporters in New York on August 25 that his son doubted he had been shot down. And three weeks later the pilot wrote the editor of the *New York Times* (letter published on September 27): "Apparently my father misunderstood the answers I gave to questions put to me during the Trial." But although "I did not see what it was that caused the explosion I feel sure that it was not the aircraft itself which exploded." Things have undoubtedly changed in Russia since Stalin's death—but not to the extent that prisoners in the Lubyanka write foreign newspapers on their own initiative.

After the Kremlin revealed the U-2 affair, Khrushchev's participation in summit negotiations might have been interpreted as a confession of weakness. Since the United States refused to admit it was wrong in violating "the Soviet Union's sovereignty," he declared in *Pravda* on June 5, "talks with President Eisenhower would have proceeded on a basis unacceptable to us—on a basis of inequality." To have engaged in negotiations without guarantees that "this aggression would not be repeated," he stated in Vienna on July 2, would have been "bowing our heads" to the aggressors. And the Soviet Premier referred to the matter as late as September 29, 1960, during his performance at the United Nations. To have crawled before President Eisenhower, he told reporters, "would have been the humiliation of my country."

By huffing and puffing, blowing down the summit, putting the United States on the defensive, and threatening its allies in the strongest terms regarding U-2 bases, Nikita Sergeyevich accomplished the almost impossible and prevented any significant diminution in Soviet prestige. Immediately after the summit fiasco, the United States Information Agency ordered a public-opinion survey. Interviewers questioned 1,150 persons in Britain and 1,000 in France between May 21 and 31. "One of the more significant elements of the U-2 incident," noted the analyst who wrote up the report,

> was the disclosure that for years the United States had been able to fly with impunity over the Soviet Union and keep a close check on military developments. This point raised the possibility that however adversely Western Europeans might be affected by other aspects of the U-2 episode, they might revise somewhat in America's favor their judgments of United States versus U.S.S.R. military might.
>
> There is little support for any such supposition in the currently available post-summit trend data. In Great Britain, the United States continues behind the U.S.S.R. by almost identically the same margin registered in February . . . In France there is a suggestion of some improvement in United States standing, but it is small in the net and still leaves the Soviet ahead.[4]

In addition to the positive arguments for acting as he did, Khrushchev had little to lose by rejecting the summit conference. After visiting the United States in the fall of 1959 and France in March and April of 1960, he could expect few additional laurels and might even lose prestige should a settlement on terms favorable to the U.S.S.R. not be forthcoming. In the eyes of the Soviet public, the U-2 incident also provided some justification for the demands that actually made a conference impossible and thus helped preserve the carefully built up picture of the Soviet Premier as a man of peace doing everything possible to relax international tensions.

On the eve of Khrushchev's departure for Paris, the Soviet press featured long accounts of mass meetings in all the principal Soviet cities and speakers denouncing the "aggressive" acts of the United States. In order to prevent any competition with such domestic propaganda, selective jamming of the Voice of America Russian-language broadcasts, suspended after the Premier's visit to the United States in 1959, resumed as early as May 16, 1960. As late as May 21, the full texts of statements by the Western leaders in Paris had not been published in the U.S.S.R. Nevertheless, according to Max Frankel of the *New York Times,* the first reaction of the Moscow public to the disruption of the summit was surprise and worry. Such phrases as "bad news" and "terrible" were heard as frequently as "Khrushchev is absolutely right."

Similarly, Nikita Sergeyevich carefully refrained from slamming any doors and apparently endeavored to absolve himself of personal responsibility before public opinion abroad. As early as May 13 rumors began to emanate from Paris that pressure from the armed forces, Peking, and Stalinists in the Soviet Communist Party would force Khrushchev to adopt a harder line. According to Charles E. Bohlen, who was present at the single short session in Paris on May 16, the Soviet Premier had said "that this was a matter that involved deeply the internal politics of the Soviet Union" (Mr. Bohlen's words, press conference of May 16[5]).

After his visit to the United States in 1959, his ostensible efforts for a *détente,* and a number of friendly public remarks about Eisenhower, the U-2 incident undoubtedly caused Khrushchev considerable personal embarrassment and probably weakened him somewhat politically. But the logic of the situation, not pressure from "hard-liners," dictated his reaction. And if he torpedoed the summit to curry favor with Peking, the effort was in vain or he had a sudden change of heart: The last issue in the U.S.S.R. of the Soviet-Chinese Friendship Society journal appeared in June 1960, and Soviet instructors and technicians were recalled from China during July. Too, by November the outside world was beginning to perceive the flat-on-face ending of Communist China's "Great Leap Forward." Even in May the Chinese could scarcely have been in a position to influence Soviet policy significantly.

Besides seeking to justify his behavior, the Soviet Premier made reassuring statements in almost every speech during May 1960 and carefully avoided any war scare. In announcing to the Supreme Soviet on May 5 that a U.S. reconnaissance plane had been shot down over Russian territory, Khrushchev declared there was no reason to consider the incident "a precursor of war or a foreshadow of attack" or even "a pre-war trial of strength." In his concluding speech to the Supreme Soviet two days later, the Premier was again careful to state that "this is so far not preparations for war, for a war of today" although it could lead to war in the future. "But this incident must not impel us to revise our plans by increasing appropriations for armaments and the army, must not impel us to halt the process of reducing the army. We shall continue to be guided by the Leninist peaceable policy, to uphold the idea of peaceful coexistence."[6] And during the impromptu press conference held on May 11 at the exhibition of the U-2 wreckage, Khrushchev remarked that he regarded "the provocative flight of the American intelligence plane over our country not as a preparation for war, but as probing."

And at Paris on May 16 he saw "no better way out than to postpone the conference of the heads of government for approximately six to eight months." He also expressed his firm belief "in the necessity of peaceful coexistence because to lose faith in peaceful coexistence would mean to doom mankind to war, would mean to agree with the inevitability of wars, and under the circumstances it is known what disasters would be brought by a war to all nations on earth."[7] Immediately after this statement, the Soviet Premier's assistants hastened to assure reporters that the Soviet Government had no intention of concluding a separate treaty with East Germany in the near future and would defer any action until after the next summit conference. The following day in East Berlin, Soviet and East German spokesmen stated categorically that Khrushchev would sign no separate treaty during his stopover in Berlin on the way home from Paris.

The Premier himself confirmed these assurances in an address in East Berlin on May 20: "Under present conditions, it is worth while to wait a little longer and try to find by joint efforts of all four victorious powers a solution of the long-since ripe question of signing a peace treaty with the two German states." And the "existing situation will apparently have to be preserved till the heads of government meeting, which, it is to be hoped, will take place in six or eight months."[8]

Khrushchev even backed his soothing words with deeds. The passengers and crew of the U.S. Army helicopter which landed in East Germany in 1958 were held for six weeks, but a U.S. Air Force transport which inadvertently wandered over East Germany on May 20, 1960 was released four days later.

4

Treaty Boil, Berlin Bubble!
(July 1960—October 1961)

IN AUGUST 1946 a group of Polish Communists met secretly in Moscow to discuss future tactics in taking over Poland. According to the account one of the participants later gave Arthur Bliss Lane, the U.S. Ambassador to Warsaw, Stalin depreciated the significance of any American protests. Opinion in the United States might become aroused over some international incident, he said, but some other matter would eventually absorb the attention of the American public. The Communists need only be patient and the United States would forget the past.[1]

But in ordering ground troops to Korea four years later, Harry Truman deposited a large fortune in the Bank of Soviet Respect for America and forced Stalin to revise his judgment. Although the Eisenhower administration drew heavily on this account for six years, the Lebanon landing in 1958 constituted a respectable deposit. And the U-2 incident also belongs on the credit side of the ledger. Confronted with Powers and the U-2 wreckage, Washington said in effect, "Yes, they're ours. And just what are you going to do about

it?" One can almost feel a certain sympathy for Nikita Sergeyevich; from his point of view it was indeed an "unpleasant situation."

And in the weeks following the abortive summit meeting
he confined himself to harsh but scarcely warlike statements.
During a visit to Austria in July 1960 he delivered several
rather ambiguous warnings—"we *may*" rather than "we *will*"
—regarding a meeting in Berlin of the lower house of the
West German Parliament scheduled for fall. In Vienna on
July 1, Khrushchev spoke with Austrian leaders. "Try to
imagine the German Federal Government suddenly having
a meeting of the Bundestag in Berlin," he said, "while at the
same time East Germany concludes a separate peace treaty
with the Soviet Union. Herr Adenauer and his Deputies
would then have to request a return visa from Herr Ulbricht.
Wouldn't that be grotesque?" At a press conference just before his departure from Vienna on July 8, the Soviet Premier
again referred to the Bundestag session: "We are going to
talk this over with Comrades Grotewohl and Ulbricht [the
East German leaders], also with representatives of other Socialist countries, and with representatives of countries that
participated in the war, to decide whether it would be possible that we also sign a peace treaty with the German Democratic Republic at the same time in September."[2] And Ulbricht was equally circumspect in his utterances. At a news
conference in East Berlin on July 19, he spoke merely of talks
being held with Soviet leaders on the matter.

Although the meeting was not actually postponed until
September 20, 1960, by the end of July it was becoming apparent that neither Bonn nor the Western powers were keen
on the idea and were attempting to "pass the buck" of re-

sponsibility for vetoing a Berlin session. On August 3 the East German Foreign Minister spoke in stronger terms: "We have declared before and we declare again that our patience is at an end and that we shall no longer tolerate such provocations."[3]

From Washington on August 2, Dana Adams Schmidt of the *New York Times* reported increasing official concern over Khrushchev's threat to sign a treaty should the Bundestag meet in Berlin: "The view was that Mr. Khrushchev had been so specific [!] in his threat, in statements in Vienna last month, that it must be assumed that he meant it. This is the interpretation that has been communicated to the West German Government. While the decision was being left to Chancellor Adenauer's Government, United States officials were making certain German officials knew about the risks they believed were involved." Nikita Sergeyevich must have found this report quite encouraging, but at a news conference on August 9, Secretary of State Herter made it practically official. "The United States Government has not taken a position on whether the Bundestag should meet in West Berlin," he said, "We feel that that is an internal matter for the Germans themselves to decide and not for us to decide."[4] And French opposition to a Berlin session was reported from both Washington and Bonn on August 22.

In the latter part of July, East German authorities detained, but later released, two trucks from West Berlin, charging that their loads of asbestos sheets were destined for the West German armed forces. But this represented the only interference worth mentioning with Berlin's four-power status or communications with West Germany during the immediate post-summit months.

Three weeks after Secretary Herter's statement, however, at midnight August 30, Communist authorities suddenly began turning back West Germans en route to West Berlin for a meeting of ex prisoners of war and a rally of persons expelled from territories occupied after World War II by Poland and the U.S.S.R. At the same time West Germans without a special entry permit were temporarily barred from East Berlin. These measures had been taken, declared a Communist announcement, to prevent misuse of East German territory "by the organization and furtherance of militaristic and irredentist agitation meetings to be held from Sept. 1 to Sept. 4 in West Berlin." The announcement also "warned" against any airlift of visitors: The Western powers would "bear the full responsibility for all consequences that may result if the air corridors are misused for the staging of agitation meetings in West Berlin."[5] Almost seven hundred of the one thousand visitors turned back at the zonal border were flown to Berlin without incident, however, and the restrictions ended at midnight September 4.

Charging a violation of East German canal regulations, on the 3rd Communist authorities had turned back four barges en route from Hamburg to Berlin. Two days later they halted twenty-three barges, claiming the water level was too low to allow their passage. And on September 8 the East-zone regime announced that West Germans would henceforth have to secure a special police permit before entering East Berlin. A few days later Communist authorities stated they would no longer recognize West German passports held by residents of West Berlin. The Apostolic Nuncio in Germany, an Italian national with diplomatic status, was barred from East Berlin on September 17; four days later the Communist paper *Neues Deutschland* declared that diplomats accredited to Bonn would need permission from the East German Foreign Ministry to enter East Germany.

Walter C. Dowling, U.S. Ambassador to West Germany, who apparently took the next train to Berlin, arrived on the morning of the 22nd. The same day, in an official car flying the American flag, he drove up to an East German control point. The police expected him.

"Diplomats accredited to Bonn cannot enter the democratic sector of Berlin," a policeman told the driver. "You must turn around and go back."

"I am the American Ambassador in Bonn," replied Mr. Dowling, "and I am also responsible for the American sector of Berlin. We consider this city open." The policeman then asked for identification and after it was produced stepped back and allowed the car to proceed.[6]

During all these efforts to compromise the four-power status of Berlin, Soviet officials said as little as possible. Apparently the idea was to disavow the East-zone regime's actions if the situation showed signs of getting out of hand but to take further steps in the absence of any strong reaction. Such tactics recall Stalin's preliminary Berlin maneuvers in 1948. They provoked no significant reaction on the part of the United States, and thus Stalin considered it safe enough to go ahead and blockade the city.

As early as September 11, the United States, Britain, and France had begun withholding travel documents for East Germans making official or semiofficial trips to the West. Such a restriction could not significantly embarrass the East-zone regime, however, and according to a report from Washington on the 12th (E. W. Kenworthy to the *New York*

Times), the United States was urging Bonn to retaliate with economic sanctions: "Unless each harassment by East Germany is promptly and effectively countered, many officials here feel the Communists will proceed until the Allies must surrender their rights in Berlin or force a showdown with the risk of war."

On September 30, 1960, Bonn gave three months' notice of its intention to abrogate the existing trade pact with East Germany. The U.S. Embassy announced "full support" of the action which the West German Government had taken after consultations with the Western powers responsible for Berlin. Reports from Washington also indicated Western approval of the move. According to an official German spokesman in Bonn, West Germany was willing to open negotiations for a new trade agreement only if West Germans were again allowed in East Berlin without special permits; East Germany must also recognize West German passports held by residents of West Berlin.

No significant Communist reaction followed this move. On October 3, East-zone authorities ceased granting transit permits for goods consigned to West Berlin from other Soviet-bloc countries, but this involved imports worth only twelve million dollars per year—goods obtainable almost as easily from the West. The East German press service announced on October 23 that West Berliners would need special police permission for each visit to cemeteries in the city's suburbs; semipermanent passes had been used previously. And at the end of the month border guards just outside Berlin seized two trucks en route to West Germany, charging that radio-teletype receivers in the cargo were "war equipment" destined for the West German armed forces.

Communist statements during October were also quite mild. On the 12th the East-zone Foreign Trade Ministry charged West Berlin authorities with sabotaging interzone trade by purchasing sand, gravel, and other building materials from Poland. Transit permits had been refused, they said, "for such goods that West Berlin authorities have refused to accept from East Germany." In an article in *Neues Deutschland* on the 17th, a Communist trade official claimed a break in interzonal trade would also cancel arrangements governing Berlin's communications with the West. "All shipments of goods to and from Berlin . . . require permits stamped by East German authorities," he wrote. "Permits have been handled generously, but this state of affairs will cease to exist when the trade pact runs out." In another article of October 30, the same official said all supplementary agreements would expire with the trade pact at the end of the year. "This includes technical arrangements for goods traffic between West Berlin and West Germany, which will then be devoid of any legal basis."

Unfortunately, Bonn failed to maintain its original unyielding attitude. To avoid provoking the Communists, the Bundestag on October 26 voted to allow the government to determine the location of the administrative headquarters of a new radio station originally intended for West Berlin. At the request of East-zone trade officials, low-level talks had started in Berlin on October 13, and Mayor Willy Brandt of West Berlin indicated that the Communists had made feelers which could lead to resumption of trade in return for guarantees of free access to the city. In a subsequent newspaper interview, however, Chancellor Adenauer said his government would assume a "flexible position" on the trade question. And in Berlin on November 25, "authoritative sources" admitted that Bonn would commence trade talks without preliminary East German concessions. "When we canceled the pact," said a West Berlin official, "there was no question of a flexible attitude." In Bonn two days later, government officials confirmed that West Germany would not insist on its original conditions for negotiation, i.e. abandonment of restrictions on West Germans entering East Berlin. Although Bonn did not demand formal repeal of the restrictions, the Communists were not expected to enforce them. "But the fact remains," reported Sydney Gruson to the *New York Times,* "that the talks will at least begin with the Communist restrictions still in effect, thus heightening the impression of some observers that Bonn, and perhaps the allies as well, have become fearful of the consequences of a halt in trade." On November 30 the West German Cabinet approved preliminary negotiations for a new trade agreement.

Encouraged by the apparent Western irresolution, Communist spokesmen soon began to use stronger words. In a speech published on December 18, Ulbricht himself made threats regarding rail traffic to West Berlin: We do not want "to play this card," he said. But there can be no doubt of serious disturbances "if the trade agreement isn't renewed."[7] And the next day a long editorial on the negotiations appeared in *Neues Deutschland*: "If no trade treaty exists by January 1, 1961, the [East] German Democratic Republic will suggest to the commandants of the occupation troops in West Berlin a special settlement for their transports."

Agreement was finally reached on December 29. According to "unimpeachable" sources in Berlin, West Germany had not insisted on official repeal of the Berlin entry restrictions, and the Communists had agreed not to enforce them. But during January 1961, East-zone police continued to stop West German autos entering East Berlin, requiring the occupants to obtain special permits, and Communist authorities still refused to recognize West German passports held by residents of West Berlin. Nevertheless, on January 19, West German officials described traffic to West Berlin as smoother than ever before, and Mayor Brandt expressed his satisfaction with the pact. On February 22, East German authorities announced a further reduction on control of traffic between Berlin and the West. Trucks would be sealed upon entering East Germany and not inspected again upon departure.

Ten days earlier, however, Communist police had turned back a number of Evangelical Church leaders who attempted to take part in an all-German service at the Marienkirche in East Berlin. East-zone authorities eased the restrictions somewhat on February 16, but police at the check points continued to issue special entry permits to West Germans crossing into East Berlin. The new measures, said Mayor Brandt, were not in accordance with the understandings on Berlin. "Western expectations for an easing of the situation were not fulfilled," said another West Berlin spokesman; "full freedom of movement has by no means been restored."

As Mátyás Rakosi, the Stalinist leader of the Hungarian Communist Party once described it, the Communists took over Hungary by means of "salami tactics," cutting away the position of the democratic parties a slice at a time. Pursuing similar tactics during the fall and winter of 1960, Khrushchev had secured a very thin slice of the West Berlin salami. Nevertheless, his basic attitude toward the United

States remained one of respectful caution; during the first months of the Kennedy administration, he even seemed to be seeking a limited but real *détente*. Within a period of two months, however, mid-April to mid-June 1961, the Soviet Premier's attitude changed completely; for a while he apparently thought he might seize the plum that even Stalin never dared pluck.

Changed circumstances in both the United States and the Soviet Union contributed to this new attitude. As late as the summer of 1958, perhaps as late as 1960, Khrushchev evidently feared a foreign-policy reverse or a serious war-scare which his opponents might use against him. By 1961, however, his position at home was secure enough in one sense to give him greater freedom abroad. Nikita Sergeyevich had finally "arrived" with respect to popular acceptance and approval. From Moscow on July 30, 1961, Seymour Topping of the *New York Times* wrote of the "father image that Mr. Khrushchev has taken on for the Soviet people. He is now quoted on every subject, from the construction of homes to the eating of horsemeat." On the anniversary of Hitler's attack on the U.S.S.R., the Soviet Premier "appeared at the Kremlin in uniform and was hailed as a leading Soviet architect of victory in World War II. Soviet cinemas are showing a lengthy documentary on the career of Mr. Khrushchev entitled 'Our Nikita Sergeyevich.'" And as early as April 1961, a town in the Ukraine had changed its name to "Khrushchev."

The situation in the United States was more complex. The fact that the guard has been changed only three times in Washington since 1933 has tended to conceal the State Department's vulnerability to new brooms. It would be too much to say that wild bulls charge through the corridors amid crashing china on these occasions, but cries of anguish are audible. In the first years of the Eisenhower administration they accompanied "Wristonization," the sometimes forced integration of civil servants into the Foreign Service; in 1961/62 they arose from a reduction in force, allegedly to reduce the Department to more manageable proportions.

A respectable number of voters value the services of practically every other federal agency, but the State Department has no constituency. It could be abolished and no one would notice the difference—except perhaps a few professors who write for such mass-circulation journals as *Foreign Affairs*. Nor does the State Department have any career official with the prestige of the armed forces chiefs or the Permanent Undersecretary at the British Foreign Office. (How many readers can name the Chiefs of Staff of the Army or Air Force or the Chief of Naval Operations? How many can name one of the two top career officers of the State Department?) A Permanent Undersecretary may be kicked upstairs, as anti-German Sir Robert Vansittart was in 1938, but even that takes time; for a few months at least he can exercise a restraining influence. Had Robert Murphy, for example, been Permanent Undersecretary at the State Department in January 1961, the Berlin wall might not exist today.

The second factor was the character of the new President. A good infantry platoon leader or PT-boat commander leads rather than commands. In carrying out his orders he asks his men to take no greater risk than he himself takes. A senior commander or head of government, on the other hand, must order men to face death while he remains in safety. A sensitive and responsible person in such a position can choose the hard alternative only when he has confidence in his staff and the conviction that the easy alternative may be fatal—such confidence and conviction come only with experience. Significantly, of the Western leaders only de Gaulle, a former general of brigade and head of a wartime government, consistently opposed negotiations on Berlin.

In offering a toast at the traditional New Year's Eve party in the Kremlin, Khrushchev set the tone for the first months of 1961. "We would like this unfortunate [U-2] incident to become a thing of the past with the departure of the old President," he said. The Soviet Government would not insist on bringing the matter before the United Nations General Assembly, he added, "so that a bad past does not hamper the hopes for a good future." And in an Inauguration Day message to President Kennedy, the Soviet Premier and Leonid Brezhnev, the titular head of state, offered congratulations and expressed "hope that by joint efforts we shall be able to attain a radical improvement of relations between our countries, to make healthier the entire international climate."[8]

The next day, January 21, Khrushchev summoned U.S. Ambassador Thompson to the Kremlin, for the first time since the preceding September. In order to "remove a serious obstacle on the road toward better Soviet-American relations," declared the Premier, he had decided to release two U.S. Air Force officers, the surviving crew members of an RB-47 shot down by a Soviet fighter over the Barents Sea on July 1, 1960. The two officers were duly released four days later.

While on a tour of Siberian agricultural regions, Khrushchev received Ambassador Thompson again at Novosibirsk on March 9. The ambassador, who had left Washington on February 23, handed over a message from President Kennedy expressing hope for an improvement in relations, and an apparently rather general discussion of four hours ensued. According to a subsequent report from Bonn, the Soviet Premier had emphasized the importance of the Berlin problem. Although stating he would not wait indefinitely for Western agreement to his proposals, he failed to mention any deadline.

During these first three months, not only Khrushchev but also the Soviet press and radio maintained a tone of marked restraint in dealing with President Kennedy. With the anti-Castro landing in Cuba, this attitude changed completely. The landing took place on April 17, and that evening *Izvestia,* the official government daily, made one of the bitterest attacks on the United States since the inauguration of the new President. It spoke of "gangs of American hirelings," "chains of American slavery," "American imperialists," and compared the Castro revolution to a "cataract in the eyes of the imperialist Yankees." At noon the next day the U.S. chargé in Moscow was called to the Foreign Ministry and given a message from Khrushchev to President Kennedy. The Soviet Premier warned against any "misunderstanding of our position: we shall render the Cuban people and their Government all necessary assistance in beating back the armed attack on Cuba." But in an official statement released at the same time, the Soviet Government demanded "the urgent study" of the landing "by the General Assembly of the United Nations." It appealed "to the Governments of all United Nations member states," and reserved the right to take, "together with other countries, all steps to render the necessary aid to the Republic of Cuba"[9] A few hours later a mob supplied with rocks and ink bottles attacked the U.S.

Embassy. Although police and troops eventually broke up the demonstration, Soviet authorities had quite clearly permitted its organization. Indeed, the embassy had been warned privately of the attack as early as 11:15 that morning.

In a second message of April 22, Khrushchev lectured the President on international ethics and U.S. "sins" against Cuba. Six days later *Pravda* attacked President Kennedy personally for the first time in what Seymour Topping called "vituperative terms that suggested a break in personal relations between him and Premier Khrushchev." "Its invective," continued the *New York Times* correspondent, "recalled the campaign of name-calling" directed against President Eisenhower after the U-2 incident. *Pravda* returned to the attack on April 30, speaking of "the hypocrisy of Kennedy's former pledges and assurances . . . Instead of the promised changes in the foreign policy of the United States, the new master of the White House preferred to follow in the footsteps of his bankrupt predecessors."

His kidneys may have bothered him, but no one ever reported that Nikita Sergeyevich's conscience kept him awake at night. To him Washington's failure to support the Cuban landing must have appeared as evidence of irresolution on the part of President Kennedy. And he can hardly have interpreted the changing U.S. policy on Laos as anything else. As early as April 7, reports from Washington spoke of Anglo-American agreement on the formation of a new government in Laos. This new government, wrote William Jorden of the *New York Times*, "would include representatives of all main elements in Laotian political life. . . . though the Western leaders were said to be hopeful that Communists could be kept out of posts that might open the way to a seizure of full power." On April 9 in Paris, U.S. Ambassador Gavin invited the self-exiled Laotian neutralist leader, Prince Souvanna Phouma, to visit Washington briefly for consultations.

In Washington the Cuban blunder seems to have caused a serious loss of confidence. By April 29, William Jorden could see no sign of a strong U.S. stand on Laos. "The President and some of his leading officials have said that the United States could hardly stand by and see Laos lost to communism," he wrote. But this attitude "has been altered of late by the addition of the proviso that those to be defended must show signs of a readiness to defend themselves." The weakness of the Royal Laotian Army had caused "undisguised disappointment here," and, although Washington hoped for a cease-fire, "serious consideration is being given to steps that might be taken to bolster the resistance and the confidence of other governments in the area."

Senator Fulbright, chairman of the Senate Foreign Relations Committee, participated in a nationally broadcast interview on April 30. "I don't think the terrain and the conditions are right for sending in our troops," he declared. "We must seek another solution, and we are." And the next day E. W. Kenworthy, a Washington correspondent of the *New York Times*, reported in a similar vein: "France is known to be opposed to any military intervention, and some other [S.E.A.T.O.] members feel strongly that Laos is not a good place for becoming involved in a 'Korea-like' action. Finally —and this, it is understood, is a compelling argument with the Administration after the failure of the rebel landings in Cuba—there is mounting opposition on Capitol Hill to sending United States troops into Laos."

Perhaps the most revealing statement was the one Secretary of State Rusk failed to make at a press conference on May 4. "Mr. Secretary," queried one reporter, "you said that the formation of a Government for the time being, at least, is a matter for the Laotians to work out. Would we accept a Communist-dominated Government, if this was something the Laotians worked out? And if we did, what happened to our idea of keeping Laos independent and neutral?" The Secretary of State bravely replied to this question but simply couldn't answer it.[10]

During the conversation with Khrushchev at Novosibirsk on March 9, Ambassador Thompson had indicated President Kennedy's favorable attitude toward an eventual summit meeting. Such a meeting was not contemplated in the near future, however, and neither time nor place was discussed. Despite the bitter tone of Soviet propaganda after the Cuban landing, Moscow reportedly revived the proposal through diplomatic channels early in May. In a speech at Erivan, capital of Soviet Armenia, on May 6, the Soviet Premier declared disarmament negotiations with the United States would take place "in a short time." Although he stated that "aggressive forces of the United States" had provoked the "attack against Cuba," Khrushchev maintained a generally mild tone and refrained from any personal reference to President Kennedy. After consulting other Western capitals, Washington responded favorably, probably sometime before May 14, and apparently suggested the date and place for the meeting. Soviet Ambassador Menshikov delivered Khrushchev's agreement on the 16th, and the pending talks were officially announced three days later.

As early as May 6, Arthur Krock reported that some members of the President's inner circle were urging a new approach to Khrushchev, perhaps a summit meeting, "to apprise and, if possible, convince Premier Khrushchev that Administration policies which revise those formerly applied to Laos and Cuba definitely do not presage the slightest yielding by the United States on holding Berlin, on the strengthening of N.A.T.O. and on all necessary resistance to the extension of Moscow-dominated governments to the Western hemisphere." Other journalists reported from Washington in similar terms, James Reston on May 15, E. W. Kenworthy on the 16th, and W. H. Lawrence on the 19th. Apparently none of the President's advisers stopped to think that Khrushchev might consider agreement to a meeting a new sign of weakness, especially after Mr. Kennedy's earlier expressed opposition to summit conferences and preference for "quiet diplomacy," the reverses in Cuba and Laos, the attack on the U.S. Embassy in Moscow, and the bitter personal attacks on the President in the Soviet press. Administration officials, wrote W. H. Lawrence, "were certain that Mr. Khrushchev, who is 67 years old, would quickly recognize Mr. Kennedy, who will be 44 May 29, as a man of decision." But most high-level conversations have to be conducted through interpreters. Presumably something was lost in the translation—English to Russian at least.

The K. and Kh. meeting took place, appropriately, in Vienna on June 3 and 4, 1961. Earlier, on April 21, Ulbricht had made new threats regarding West Berlin, the first major verbal attack by the Communists since the preceding year. At the end of that month Moscow also withdrew the major general commanding the Soviet garrison in East Berlin. Since his successor was a colonel, a lower rank than that of the

Western commandants in Berlin, this move in effect denied the four-power status of the city. And at Vienna Khrushchev handed over a lengthy memorandum on Germany and disarmament.

"If the United States does not show an understanding of the necessity of concluding a peace treaty," it stated, "we would have to sign a peace treaty . . . with those that want to sign it." The U.S.S.R. and other signatories would respect West Berlin's subsequent status as a "free city," but the treaty would "mean the liquidation of the occupation regime in West Berlin with all consequences arising therefrom. Specifically, the questions of using land, water and air communications across the territory of the German Democratic Republic will have to be settled not otherwise than through appropriate agreement with the German Democratic Republic." This, of course, represented nothing new—everything had been said before.

Nor did the memorandum establish any deadline for the actual signing of the treaty: "In order not to drag out the peace settlement it is necessary to establish deadlines *within which the Germans must explore the possibilities of agreements on questions falling into their internal competence* [italics supplied]. The Soviet Government regards a period not exceeding six months adequate for such talks. This period is fully adequate for contact between the Federal Republic of Germany and the Democratic Republic of Germany and for talks between them."[11] Nikita Sergeyevich evidently wanted an additional sign of Western hesitation; had Washington displayed a resolute attitude at this juncture he might well have decided to let the Berlin crisis simmer away as it had been simmering ever since November 1958.

Although the policy of the United States toward the planned meeting of the Bundestag had not proven too accurate as a political barometer in 1960, conditions had changed and a similar maneuver, deliberate this time, might provoke a more reliable reaction. And at the time Bonn was apparently considering a meeting of the upper house of its Parliament, the Bundesrat, in Berlin on June 16. Thus on June 8, four days after the Vienna talks, the Soviet Foreign Ministry delivered formal notes to the British, French, U.S., and West German embassies. A Berlin session of the Bundesrat, the notes to the Western powers declared, would "aggravate the situation in this city, which is abnormal as it is. The peace-loving forces, naturally, cannot tolerate such a situation." The Soviet Government expected the Western authorities, "now bearing definite responsibility for the situation in West Berlin," to "take necessary measures, ruling out the above dangerous actions, with regard to West Berlin." The note addressed to Bonn closed on a somewhat stronger tone: "All responsibility for the consequences arising from the organization of demonstrations hostile to the cause of peace in West Berlin will rest wholly with the Government of the Federal Republic of Germany and also with those who patronize them."[12]

The next day in Bonn, Dr. Franz Meyers, President of the Bundesrat, admitted that a June 16 session in Berlin had been contemplated but claimed the idea had been abandoned before Moscow had protested. This was probably true even though a report from Berlin on June 11 stated that Dr. Meyers "announced his intention in Bonn, meanwhile, to cancel the Berlin meeting." Whether the meeting was canceled before or after the protest, the Bundesrat did *not* meet in Berlin. But in the U.S. Senate on the 14th, Senator Mike Mansfield, the Democratic majority leader, urged a free-city status for Berlin with the United Nations or some other international agency responsible for its protection. Continuation of the status quo would lead to war, he said. Although the senator stated he spoke only as an individual, Russell Baker of the *New York Times* noted the fear of some officials "that Europeans, who have difficulty understanding the loose-knit structure of American government in the best of times, would read the Mansfield speech as a harbinger of change in Administration policy on Berlin."

Khrushchev can hardly be blamed for drawing the logical conclusion, that the United States Government would back down in the face of an outright ultimatum. And he delivered it in the course of a television speech on June 15: "We ask everyone to understand us correctly: The conclusion of a peace treaty with Germany cannot be postponed any longer. A peaceful settlement in Europe must be attained this year." Six days later the Soviet Premier appeared at a special meeting in the Kremlin in the uniform of a lieutenant general, his wartime rank as a political officer, and in a speech broadcast over the Moscow radio and television repeated the ultimatum in stronger terms: "at the end of this year, we, together with other peace-loving states, will sign a peace treaty with the German Democratic Republic. . . . As regards those who try to threaten us with war if we sign a peace treaty with the German Democratic Republic, they will bear the entire responsibility for their actions."[13] Ludicrous as the idea might once have seemed, Nikita Sergeyevich could even follow salami tactics in presenting ultimatums.

The issue of *Newsweek* which appeared on the stands

June 26 contained reports of the measures the Joint Chiefs of
Staff intended to recommend to President Kennedy in connection with the impending Berlin crisis. They included
evacuation of American dependents from Europe, calling up
four National Guard divisions and movement of one or more
divisions to Europe, and resumption of nuclear testing. According to a June 30 dispatch from Jack Raymond, a Washington correspondent of the *New York Times,* the reports
rested on information furnished openly by several government departments, presumably in the week preceding the
26th. If so this might account for the somewhat milder tone
Khrushchev adopted in a message to Ulbricht, a message the
East German press agency published on June 28: A peace
treaty was long overdue, said the Soviet Premier, and "the
Soviet Union together with all other peace-loving nations
will do their utmost [italics supplied] to sign one by the end
of this year."[14] Although devoting much of a Kremlin speech
two days later to the problem of Germany, Khrushchev refrained from mentioning any deadline. And he attended the
traditional July 4 party at the U.S. Embassy in a very
friendly mood, accompanied by Mikoyan, Marshal Malinovsky, and some five hundred other important Soviet citizens.

On July 11 Deputy Secretary of Defense Roswell L. Gilpatric disclosed that the Department of Defense was considering mobilizing certain National Guard and Army Reserve
units. Five days later administration officials said that the
President would probably declare a limited national emergency. And in a television speech to the nation on July 25,
Mr. Kennedy announced a number of measures to meet the
crisis: increases in the regular strength of the armed forces,
doubling and tripling of draft calls, a request to Congress for

authority to call up units and individuals of the reserve, extensive new civil defense preparations, and increased defense spending.

Khrushchev received news of this speech as he was conferring with John J. McCloy, the President's disarmament adviser, at Sochi on the Black Sea—and immediately flew into a "foot-stamping, bellowing rage."[15] If this "rage" was real rather than assumed, the Premier soon had second thoughts. In private conversations as early as July 19, reported Seymour Topping from Moscow, Soviet officials had betrayed concern over the Berlin crisis getting out of control. The Soviet press also complained about the growing "war psychosis" in the United States. "A military hysteria is now being drummed up in the United States," charged Khrushchev in an address of August 7. "At the same time, there are some who are conditioning the American people to the idea that there would be nothing particularly terrible even if war does break out."[16] The Soviet Premier may really have feared an aroused public opinion in the United States, a development which would have precluded any concessions by the West. Although maintaining pressure upon Washington during the subsequent months, he repeatedly addressed soothing statements and gestures to Western public opinion.

"The Soviet Union was and is ready for talks both on the German question and all other outstanding issues," declared *Pravda* on July 19.

Although "ready to defend our interests," replied President Kennedy in his speech of July 25, "we shall also be ready to search for peace—in quiet exploratory talks, in formal or informal meetings."

The Soviet Premier took up the theme in earnest on August 2 when Italian Premier Fanfani and Foreign Minister Segni arrived in Moscow for a state visit. "We believe that there will be no war," Khrushchev told them. "A German peace treaty is necessary, and so are negotiations." The next day the Soviet Foreign Ministry delivered long, parallel notes on Berlin to the French, British, U.S., and West German embassies. The note to the U.S. Embassy failed to mention any deadline but stated that "the Soviet Government declares again that it is ready for talks aimed at the conclusion of a German peace treaty." And the Soviet Premier stressed this point in concluding the radio and television address of August 7: "The Soviet Union does not want to go to war with anyone. . . . This is why we address the Governments of the United States of America, Britain and France once more: Let us honestly meet at a round-table conference, let us not create a war psychosis, let us clear the atmosphere, let us rely on reasons and not on the power of thermonuclear weapons."

But before embarking on a major soothing-syrup campaign in the West, Nikita Sergeyevich had to pay the price for his earlier, more belligerent utterances. The steady draining away of the ablest and most productive elements of the East German population through West Berlin had long been a serious problem for the East-zone authorities. And after Khrushchev's deadline and harsh statements in June aroused fears that the Berlin escape hatch might soon be closed, the stream of defectors threatened to grow to a flood. During the first twelve days of July, over eight thousand persons fled to West Berlin, and by the 13th they were arriving at the rate of over a thousand per day. On the 22nd Communist authorities instituted police controls on trains entering Berlin from East Germany, but it was estimated that they succeeded in turning back only about thirty per cent of the fugitives. By the end of the month, defectors had to pass at least three check points: upon boarding a train in East Germany, at the first station in East Berlin, and just before leaving East Berlin. Ernst Lemmer, West German Minister for All-German Affairs, estimated that the police halted every other person seeking to escape. Although he termed it a "mystery that so many refugees still reach West Berlin," 1,926 managed to do so during the twenty-four hours ending at 4:00 P.M., August 9.

One might argue that the Soviet Premier had deliberately built up tension over Berlin to reduce the chances of a dangerous Western reaction when he did seal off the Eastern sector of the city, i.e. to cause Paris, London, and Washington to greet the action with relief rather than alarm. Although this is exactly what happened, Khrushchev's earlier behavior hardly supports the theory that he deliberately planned it that way. Instead of following long-term plans, he tended to meet each situation as it developed.

Mikhail A. Menshikov, Soviet Ambassador to Washington, sailed for home on July 20. Ten days later Khrushchev called Ambassador Andrei A. Smirnov home from Bonn (the ambassador had returned from vacation and consultations with senior officials of the Soviet Foreign Ministry three weeks earlier). Presumably the Soviet Premier wished to consult the two ambassadors before sealing off the Eastern sector of Berlin. He evidently reached his decision sometime between July 31 and August 2, and the Party First Secretaries of the other Warsaw Pact countries, i.e. the European satellites, met in Moscow from the 3rd to the 5th to hear the order of the day. On August 8 the East German news agency announced a meeting of the East-zone parliament scheduled for the 12th; on the 10th it disclosed that Marshal Ivan S. Konev had assumed command of Soviet forces in East Germany. Finally, early in the morning of August 13, 1961, truckloads of Communist police with sirens screaming sped through Berlin to the sector border and sealed off the Eastern part of the city.

While taking this action the Soviet Premier specifically if indirectly disavowed any intention of infringing the status of West Berlin. At a Kremlin reception for a visiting Rumanian delegation on the 11th, he had made a point of mixing with Western ambassadors present. In an affable mood, he reportedly expressed his belief in the solution of the Berlin problem through negotiations. He also mentioned that he planned to leave Moscow on the weekend, of the 12–13th, for a vacation at Sochi on the Black Sea. The implication Khrushchev apparently wished to convey was that any moves and developments during his absence should not be regarded as really serious. "It goes without saying," declared an August 13 communiqué of the Warsaw Pact powers, "that these measures must not affect the existing order of traffic and control on the ways of communication between West Berlin and Western Germany." And the East German decree issued the same day also emphasized the theme: "This decree in no way revises former decisions on transit between West Berlin and West Germany via the German Democratic Republic." Three days later Soviet Ambassador Smirnov assured Chancellor Adenauer that Khrushchev planned no moves which would make the Berlin situation worse; he was also willing to delay talks on the issue until after the West German election of September 17.

Nikita Sergeyevich had one more unpleasant chore to perform before putting the campaign for an ostensible *détente* in high gear: a new series of nuclear tests, the first since 1958. We can only speculate on his exact motives for this move. Soviet scientists may have had no more new weapons to test by 1958—may have needed several years to evaluate the earlier tests and design new weapon systems. And after the West failed to react to the partition of Berlin, Khrushchev may have hoped he could resume testing without starting a nuclear arms race. If such was the case, he would have wanted to start the tests as soon as possible after sealing off East Berlin, i.e. to complete all his dirty work at one time.

Alternatively and more likely, the Soviet Premier may have timed the test series to coincide with the stand-down on Berlin in order to obscure this indubitable retreat. Nikita Sergeyevich considered Soviet prestige far more important than the reaction of World Public Opinion to Soviet policies and moves. As Stalin put it, "How many divisions has the Pope?" Although it shouldn't be accepted literally, one passage of Khrushchev's speech of August 7 probably reflected a very real concern: "If we renounce the conclusion of a peace treaty, they would regard this as a strategic break-through and would widen the range of their demands at once. They would demand the liquidation of the Socialist system in the German Democratic Republic."

On August 31, 1961 the Soviet Government announced the resumption of testing; the first shot of the new series was fired almost immediately. Prestige considerations had obviously dictated a number of passages in the official announcement of the 31st: Rejecting the thesis of "brush fire" wars, the announcement declared that "any armed conflict, even insignificant at first, would inevitably grow into a universal rocket and nuclear war should the nuclear powers have been drawn into it." Under these circumstances, the Soviet Government "would have not fulfilled its sacred duty . . . had it not used the available possibilities for perfecting the most effective types of weapons that can cool the hotheads in the capitals of some NATO powers. The Soviet Union has worked out designs for creating a series of super powerful nuclear bombs of 20, 30, 50 and 100 million tons of T.N.T. and powerful rockets, similar to those with the help of which Maj. Y. A. Gagarin and Maj. G. S. Titov made their unrivalled cosmic flights around the earth, can lift and deliver such nuclear bombs to any point on the globe wherefrom an attack on the Soviet Union or other Socialist countries could be launched."[17]

On the eve of the new tests, Nikita Sergeyevich opened, or rather opened wider, the soothing-syrup spigot. In "private and informal exchanges" with Western ambassadors, reported Seymour Topping from Moscow on August 24, high Soviet officials had urged a Western offer of negotiations. "Their position is that Premier Khrushchev, in his recent speeches, has given adequate notice of his willingness to participate in an East-West conference on Berlin and Germany." In a message delivered to Italian Premier Fanfani the same day, the Soviet Premier expressed his willingness to negotiate with the Western powers over Berlin. He also urged early negotiations during a series of talks with columnist Drew Pearson. Nikita Sergeyevich made one especially interesting and perhaps significant remark to Pearson: "I came to have admiration for [Secretary of State] Dulles before he died. He would disagree with you, but *you knew exactly where he stood* [italics supplied]."[18]

On August 31 the Soviet Premier received two left-wing members of the British Labour Party. He indicated his desire for negotiations and stated he was resuming nuclear tests to compel the Western powers to agree to talks. In a letter delivered to Premier Fanfani two days later, Khrushchev again stated his readiness to negotiate.

"Who's next, please? Mr. C. L. Sulzberger of the *New York Times*? Step right in, Mr. Sulzberger. Comrade Khrushchev has your interview ready." This audience took place on September 5, and Nikita Sergeyevich said he would be willing to meet again with President Kennedy.

In a Kremlin speech three days later, the Soviet Premier began to back down on the year-end deadline for a German peace treaty. He referred to a statement by President Kennedy at a press conference on August 30, that the United States was prepared to "participate in any exchange of views" through "all available channels" to explore the possibility of a peaceful solution. "If this reflects the real intentions of the Western powers," said Khrushchev, "if they are ready for business-like negotiations, the Soviet Government welcomes this. . . . But it is impossible to put off a peaceful settlement with Germany to infinity. And if anyone expects to use the talk about negotiations in order to gain time, to mislead public opinion, I should like to say quite definitely once more this will not succeed." The Soviet Premier also complained about the "war hysteria" he claimed was being whipped up in the United States.[19] In a message to a meeting of the Inter-Parliamentary Union in Brussels on September 13, he again expressed his government's readiness to participate in a conference on Germany, but such a conference must "not be used to delay conclusion of a German peace treaty."

Early in September, Khrushchev invited Paul-Henri Spaak, Belgian Foreign Minister and former Secretary General of N.A.T.O., to visit Moscow. M. Spaak accepted the invitation and spoke with the Soviet Premier for three hours on the 19th. During this conversation, Khrushchev reportedly said he would set no time limit on negotiations and had never meant to establish a year-end deadline for talks.[20] Soviet Foreign Minister Gromyko spoke with Secretary of State Rusk in New York on September 21, 27, and 30. In the third conversation he too indicated that his government would not necessarily hold to the year-end deadline. And during the first week of October the Soviet press adopted a noticeably milder tone. From Moscow on October 7, Seymour Topping wrote of "what looked like a deliberate cutback in the publication of reports on military measures being taken by the Western powers. These had been given prominence by the Soviet press, radio and television as preparations for an attack on the Soviet Union." Finally, in his address opening the Twenty-Second Congress of the Soviet Communist Party on October 17, Khrushchev formally withdrew the deadline: "The Soviet Government as before insists on the speediest solution of the German problem, it is against putting it off to infinity. If the Western powers display readiness to settle the German problem, the question of the time limit for the signing of a German peace treaty will not be so material; we shall not insist that the peace treaty be signed by all means before Dec. 31, 1961."[21]

Although President Kennedy's vigorous defense measures and the "war hysteria" in the United States were probably the main factors, domestic political considerations in the U.S.S.R. may also have dictated a stand-down. In his dispatch of October 7, Seymour Topping had reported "a feeling among Western observers that the new tone [of the Soviet press] was further aimed at reassuring the Soviet people. As a danger of war had appeared to grow more acute over the recent weeks, signs of uneasiness had multiplied among the population."

A war scare definitely existed in Poland during the latter part of August and the first part of September. Panic buying and hoarding started after the sealing off of East Berlin and grew worse after the Soviet Union resumed nuclear testing. By September 5, sugar, flour, and salt were almost unobtainable in Warsaw stores, and four days later the scare-buying had extended to canned goods, watches, and jewelry. Despite large-scale emergency deliveries on the 10th and 11th, queues were still evident throughout Warsaw on the 12th.

Russians are somewhat more effectively sealed off from outside information than are the Poles. Nevertheless, many members of the Soviet middle class, factory managers, government and Party officials, etc., must have been able to read a rather disturbing message between the lines of the official propaganda. And despite his acceptance, his "legitimacy," Nikita Sergeyevich still had to respect the fears and opinions of these people. In giving Stalin's bones another kick during the Twenty-Second Party Congress and removing his body from the mausoleum on Red Square, Khrushchev was attempting to curry additional favor with the class which suffered most from the old tyrant's terror. And the more politically sophisticated Soviet citizens must have interpreted their Premier's attack on Albania and the resultant sudden departure of Chou En-lai from the Party congress as a rejection of the belligerent foreign policy advocated by Peking.

Although October 17 marked the end of Khrushchev's first Berlin crisis, he apparently still hoped to gain by cajolery what he had failed to secure through bluff and bluster. In the interview of September 5, the Premier had asked C. L. Sulzberger to tell President Kennedy that he would like to establish some sort of personal, informal contact in order to exchange views on ways to solve the Berlin problem. But Khrushchev seemed to expect an agreement more or less on Soviet terms: The President, he said, could "express his opinions on the various forms and stages of a settlement and how to prepare public opinion so as not to endanger Kennedy's prestige and that of the United States."

Mr. Sulzberger conveyed the message to McGeorge Bundy of the White House staff in a letter sent from Paris by a special diplomatic courier on September 9. When this overture failed to elicit an early reply, Mikhail A. Kharlamov, then the press chief of the Soviet Foreign Ministry, who had accompanied Gromyko to a meeting of the U.N. General Assembly, gave Pierre Salinger, the President's press secretary, a similar message on September 23. Mr. Salinger read the Soviet official Kennedy's cordial but noncommittal reply the next day. Then on the 29th a 26-page personal letter from Khrushchev to the President arrived in the United States.

This was the beginning of an extensive personal correspondence that lasted until Kennedy's death two years later. The regular "postman" on the Soviet side was a nondiplomat, Georgi N. Bolshakov, who was attached to the embassy in Washington as editor of the magazine USSR—and was also a senior agent of the K.G.B., the Soviet security police. When he delivered the first letter to Mr. Salinger, he declared that in the United States only he and Gromyko knew about it; not even Soviet Ambassador Menshikov had been informed. Bolshakov delivered most of the subsequent letters, in a conspiratorial manner on street corners or in bars, to the press secretary. When Mr. Salinger was unavailable, he would contact Attorney General Robert Kennedy, Theodore C. Sorensen, the President's speech writer, or another White House staff member. And on January 18, 1962, the press secretary received an official and Robert Kennedy an unofficial invitation to visit Moscow. The President and his brother agreed that the latter should not go to Russia, but Mr. Salinger made the visit in May and had several long talks with the Soviet Premier.

In September 1961 Mr. Sulzberger suspected that Khrushchev really wanted to offer concessions which might be opposed by Soviet Foreign Ministry officials and thus wished to avoid contacts through regular diplomatic channels. It seems more likely, however, that Nikita Sergeyevich meant exactly what he said when Sulzberger urged him to send the message through the U.S. Ambassador. "Thompson is very able but he is an Ambassador," replied the Soviet Premier. "He would have to send such a message to Secretary Rusk. Rusk would tell Kennedy what was wrong with it before he told him what the message was and Kennedy would end up wearing Rusk's corset." In other words, if one could deal directly with that Kennedy kid or his amateur assistants, by-passing his professional advisers, one might still cozen him out of most of his marbles.[22]

This approach didn't work either. In the meantime, however, a new development at the end of October 1961 encouraged Khrushchev to try his bluff and bluster tactics once again.

5

Back to the Old Salami Slicer
(August 1961–March 1962)

F ROM Washington on August 15, Max Frankel could report no strong official reaction to the Soviet partition of Berlin. "As long as Western rights of access to the divided city
are respected," the highest administration officials said "protest and vigorous propaganda will be their primary form of
retaliation." In a speech on the 14th, Chancellor Adenauer
had mentioned the possibility of a trade embargo. But three
days later Ernst Lemmer, Minister for All-German Affairs,
admitted that the Allies had not agreed on such a measure;
an embargo by only one country would have little effect.

On the 16th, however, Mayor Willy Brandt sent a personal letter to President Kennedy: "The development has not
changed the determination of the West Berlin population to
defend themselves, but it was apt to arouse doubts about the
Western powers' ability to react and about their determination," he wrote. "Inactivity and mere defensive tactics could
bring about a crisis in confidence toward the West. . . . We
might then witness a flight out of Berlin instead of a flight to
Berlin." The mayor suggested several measures and in con-

clusion said he would "welcome it if the American garrison would demonstratively receive some reinforcement."[1] Two days later the President ordered an additional battle group (a beefed-up rifle battalion) to Berlin, and the same evening (of the 18th) Vice President Johnson and General Lucius D. Clay, retired, U.S. Commander in Europe at the time of the 1948/49 airlift, took off for the divided city.

The 1st Battle Group of the 18th Infantry, 8th Division, arrived in West Berlin via the autobahn on August 20. Although only a token force, it consisted of fifteen hundred well-trained and well-equipped infantrymen rather than press releases or notes of protest. Sydney Gruson witnessed their arrival: "A roar went up from the crowd, echoing down the road and rising in volume as the crowd sighted the soldiers. Flowers came from everywhere. The troops, in battledress on their trucks, first looked astounded, then embarrassed, then delighted. . . . The crowds broke through the police lines and the whole convoy was held up as the police tried to clear a way. Again and again the scene was repeated. . . . Later the troops paraded through parts of the city, along streets lined five deep with enthusiastic watchers." And General Clay, well-remembered as the architect of the airlift, was cheered at every appearance.

According to an Associated Press report from Washington on August 23, the reception accorded General Clay had deeply impressed the Vice President who was urging that he be brought back into the government in an active role. And at his press conference on August 30, President Kennedy announced the general's appointment as "my personal representative in Berlin with the rank of Ambassador." General Clay arrived back in Berlin on September 19 and received another enthusiastic welcome. Berliners, in places three deep, waving hats and handkerchiefs lined most of the ten-mile route to his guest-house residence.

At the Friedrichstrasse crossing point, the only one left open for foreigners entering East Berlin, Communist police on August 22 had held a U.S. Army major and three sergeants when they entered the Eastern sector in an official car. An American liaison officer soon arrived on the scene, however, and secured their release with little trouble. The first direct and deliberate challenge to Allied rights in the city occurred two days later when Communist police turned back three busloads of U.S. troops starting on a sightseeing tour of East Berlin. But the buses returned a few hours later after American military police had joined the infantry detachment at the crossing point. When they were halted a second time, Lt. Col. Robert Sabolyk, provost marshal of the U.S. Berlin Command, walked across the border and gave the East-zone police a half-hour to get a Soviet officer to the scene. No Soviet officer appeared, but on the thirtieth minute the police allowed the buses to proceed. The next day three more busloads of troops crossed at the same point without incident.

At 3:55 P.M. on the 30th, Communist police halted an American captain and three sergeants in a car about three-quarters of a mile inside East Berlin. Fifty minutes later, three Patton tanks and an infantry platoon in five armored personnel carriers clattered up to the Friedrichstrasse crossing, apparently prepared to go to the rescue of the four soldiers. Twenty minutes after this development, however, the four drove back through the crossing point with nothing worse than a broken window.

A lull followed until September 21 when East-zone police halted two American soldiers traveling from West Berlin to West Germany via the autobahn. The soldiers were taken to Potsdam where the police held them for six hours until a Soviet officer ordered their release. The next day the U.S. Army instituted regular military police patrols on the autobahn, six patrols every twenty-four hours. Two days later, on the 24th, Colonel Andrei I. Solovyev, the Soviet commander in Berlin, personally delivered to Major General Albert E. Watson, the American commander, a written "warning" from Marshal Konev regarding the patrols. The marshal took no other action, however, and the patrols and traffic on the autobahn continued without incident.

The next nibble occurred on October 15; when the occupants refused to show identity cards, Communist police halted four cars attempting to enter East Berlin. Although drivers and passengers wore civilian clothes, the vehicles carried U.S. military license plates, which the East-zone authorities had accepted as identification in the past. A week later, E. Allan Lightner, Jr., a Foreign Service officer and assistant chief of the American mission in Berlin, attempted to drive into East Berlin with his wife in a private auto with official license plates. East German guards halted the car and asked for identification; Mr. Lightner refused to produce any and asked that a Soviet officer be brought to the scene. After waiting for about thirty-five minutes, Mr. Lightner again attempted to proceed and was again halted, this time some forty yards inside Communist territory. The time was now about 7:50 P.M., and Mr. Lightner sat in the car, surrounded by East-zone police, until 9:00 P.M. when Colonel Sabolyk ordered a lieutenant and eight military policemen across the border. The Communist police merely stepped back and stared, and the detachment escorted the two Americans back across the line without incident. Meanwhile four U.S. tanks and two armored personnel carriers had moved up to a position approximately five hundred yards from the Friedrichstrasse crossing point.

After leaving his wife in West Berlin, Mr. Lightner again attempted to enter the Eastern sector and was again stopped. This time the military police escorted him some two hundred yards into East Berlin and back. When he crossed the border a third time at 10:10 P.M., East-zone police allowed the car to pass. Subsequently during the evening several other civilian vehicles with official plates entered East Berlin without being halted.

Although no autos were stopped the following day, the 23rd, the East German Interior Ministry announced that all foreigners entering East Berlin must show passports. At 7:30 A.M. on the 25th, Communist police again halted an auto whose passengers were in civilian clothes and refused to identify themselves. About an hour later three armored personnel carriers and several jeeps with military policemen drove up to the American side of the border. When the East-zone police halted a second car at 10:45, twelve military policemen escorted the vehicle two hundred yards into East Berlin and back. At the same time the U.S. garrison in West Berlin was put on a general alert, and at 11:15 ten American tanks advanced to within a few yards of the crossing point while the British moved three tanks and a company of infantry to the vicinity of the Brandenburg Gate. That afternoon General Watson, the American commander, made a fruitless protest to his Soviet opposite number, Colonel Solovyev, and late in the afternoon the U.S. forces withdrew from the immediate vicinity of the border.

The next day, October 26, saw a somewhat similar performance. At about 1:00 P.M. an American liaison officer notified Soviet authorities in East Berlin that an American in civilian clothes would drive into the Eastern sector of the city in an auto bearing the official plates issued for nonmilitary vehicles; the U.S. authorities requested that a Soviet officer be sent to the crossing point to handle any necessary identification check. At 3:00 P.M. three tanks moved up to the American side of the border at the Friedrichstrasse. A few minutes later the American in civilian clothes crossed the border and was halted a few yards within East Berlin. "They went through what has now become a ritual," reported Sydney Gruson. "The policeman asked for the American's documents. The American refused and demanded that a Soviet officer be brought to the scene." Colonel Sabolyk finally walked over, got in the car, and rode back to the border where he too asked for a Soviet officer. A police captain said the decision on calling for one was up to his superiors. "That means no," replied the colonel, and he added, "We are coming over. Tell that to your superiors." Escorted by three jeeploads of soldiers with fixed bayonets, the auto crossed the border a second time. The jeeps accompanied it for a block, and the car cruised on its own for about five minutes. The East-zone police halted it again on its return, but the jeeps again crossed the border and escorted it back to West Berlin.

Late that evening, thirty-three Soviet tanks moved into the center of East Berlin and parked about a mile from the Friedrichstrasse crossing point. The following day, October 27, 1961, nothing happened until a few minutes after 4:00

P.M. when West Berlin police began clearing civilians from the street near the crossing point. At 4:20 five jeeploads of military police, ten tanks, and five armored personnel carriers drove up to the American side of the border. A few minutes later two Americans in civilian clothes attempted to drive through in an Army-licensed Volkswagen. East German police halted them, but stepped aside when the military police in jeeps escorted the vehicle over the border. Once across, the car went a block on its own and upon returning was once again escorted over the line by the jeeps.

The whole demonstration lasted about four minutes, and when it was over the American tanks began to withdraw. The last ones departed at 4:50, but at 4:55 ten Soviet medium tanks clattered up to the crossing point. The military police in the five jeeps raced back to the scene. "But with no tanks on the other side," reported Sydney Gruson, "the Soviet armor withdrew. Five minutes later the American tanks were back and thirty minutes after that so were the Russian tanks." The two tank forces remained in position during the night, but at 10:30 the next morning the Soviet armor began withdrawing from the immediate vicinity and the Americans followed suit about an hour later.

"The Americans were expected to continue sending their officials in civilian dress into East Berlin," reported Sydney Gruson on the evening of the 27th when the tanks of both powers were still in position. "If the Russians stop them—and this is the Americans' hope—no effort is likely to be made to get them through with force. . . . The point the Americans were seeking to establish was that the East Germans had no right to control Allied personnel in or out of uniform."

As night fell on the 27th, General Clay was in an excellent

position to establish this point. He had only to send an official over the line in civilian clothes the next morning. Had the official demanded that a Soviet officer be summoned, the East-zone police were scarcely in a position to refuse as several Soviet officers were present with the tank force. When the Communist police halted two British military busses two days later, a British officer accompanied by two policemen walked over to three Soviet officers sitting in a car just inside East Berlin. But as he approached, the driver hastily drove away. The Soviet tank unit appeared and reappeared rather tardily on the 27th, and Soviet authorities were apparently still worrying about General Clay's potentialities as late as November 11: The First Secretary of the Soviet Embassy in East Berlin told Western diplomats that the Brandenburg Gate on the border of the British sector might be opened as a crossing point for foreigners since it was "more representative." Presumably the Friedrichstrasse crossing on the border of the American sector would have been closed. And on November 19, East German troops and workmen began erecting tank obstacles at strategic points behind the border wall.

Six months later, Khrushchev indirectly admitted to Pierre Salinger that he personally had been the first to lose his nerve: He had held an emergency consultation with Defense Minister Malinovsky, said the Premier. "West Berlin means nothing to us, so I told Malinovsky to back up our tanks a little bit and hide them behind buildings where the Americans couldn't see them. If we do this, I said to Malinovsky, the American tanks will also move back within twenty minutes and we will have no more crisis."[2]

But General Clay really should have known that he couldn't get away with anything so un-American, so un-too-little-and-too-late, as calling the Soviet bluff. As early as October 26, Washington seemed more hopeful than resolute. "The belief here [in Washington] is that the Soviet Union will not permit the East German regime to close the one remaining crossing point," wrote E. W. Kenworthy. "In fact, there is some confidence that . . . Moscow may decide not to press the issue of identification by the East German police." Because of the time difference, news of the appearance of the Soviet tanks at the border probably reached Washington during the afternoon of the 27th. "For the moment," reported Max Frankel that evening, State Department officials "were content to accept the acknowledgement of Soviet responsibility in East Berlin and to await an indication of how the Russians intended to meet their responsibility." And during the evening of the 27th Washington evidently ordered General Clay to make no further efforts to send officials in civilian clothes into East Berlin.

By the 28th the retreat was painfully apparent: "The administration proclaimed itself satisfied that Moscow had accepted responsibility for East German interference with Allied traffic at the border," wrote Max Frankel. "There were indications here [in Washington] that armed soldiers would not be sent into East Berlin in the next few days. . . . It was said that the Allies might consider accepting the identification-card procedure if the Russians would reopen some of the Allied entrances to East Berlin that they sealed last August." In Berlin on the 28th, for the first time in four days, U.S. authorities made no effort to send an official in civilian clothes across the line.

Nikita Sergeyevich again drew the obvious conclusion and promptly ordered a new slice-by-slice campaign. On four occasions during the weekend of the 28–29th, East-zone police refused to recognize the usual diplomatic passes tendered by members of the U.S. mission in Berlin and demanded passports instead. A few days later they also rejected four-power documents shown by the deputy chiefs of the Danish and Norwegian military missions in Berlin. On November 3 and 4, Communist police halted four U.S. Army vehicles carrying uniformed soldiers on a routine patrol of East Berlin. East Berlin police detained two British tourists for four and a half hours and two British civil servants for nine hours on November 15. In East Berlin on December 3, police broke the radio aerials on two U.S. Army sedans and smashed a tail light on a third. On December 8, East German workmen erected regular customs-barrier gates at the crossing points; three days later even military vehicles had to halt for a brief inspection before entering the Eastern sector of the city. On December 21, Communist police refused to admit a State Department official en route to a prearranged meeting at the Soviet headquarters in East Berlin. Finally, on December 23, the American commander, General Watson, canceled an appointment with his Soviet opposite number when the border guards demanded identification from the three civilian aids accompanying him.

But interference with communications to West Germany were potentially much more serious. On October 29, the day after the American back-down, a Soviet officer turned back two of the American military police patrols on the autobahn. Two more were halted on the 30th, and the U.S. Army abandoned official patrols the same day. But by November 4, Soviet officers at the autobahn check points were reportedly demanding that U.S. Army drivers declare they were not on patrol missions. Just outside West Berlin on December 8, Soviet officers held up two American convoys for an hour and a half each. And three days later East-zone authorities began to delay civilian trucks leaving West Berlin; a back-up of more than a hundred trucks en route to West Germany lasted until the morning of the 12th.

At Marienborn, just across the zonal border from West Germany, Soviet authorities on November 23 had detained for fifteen hours an American military passenger train en route from West Berlin to Frankfurt. The train was allowed to proceed only upon the surrender of an East German who had concealed himself aboard at a stop in East Germany. On December 10 the East-zone railway administration restricted West Berlin traffic to two tracks, one for freight and one for passenger trains. Before the month was out, Allied military trains were being delayed as much as three hours.

Although this harassment of surface communications to West Berlin continued, Nikita Sergeyevich evidently considered it advisable to administer a fresh dose of soothing syrup to Western public opinion before attempting to slice the other end of the West Berlin salami, the city's air communications with the West. Thus, early in January 1962, Soviet authorities indicated their willingness to exchange Francis Gary Powers, the U-2 pilot, for Colonel Rudolf Abel, a Soviet spy serving a prison sentence in the United States. East German authorities released two American college students on January 15; the two, Victor Pankey and Gilbert Ferrey, had been sentenced in September to two years in prison after attempting to smuggle a woman out of East Berlin. Finally, on February 10, Powers and Abel were traded in Berlin. Included in the exchange was Frederic L. Pryor, an American graduate student studying in West Berlin who had been arrested in East Berlin on August 25.

The next day Max Frankel began a dispatch from Washington with "What ever happened to the 'Berlin crisis'?" But the question was purely rhetorical. On February 7 the Soviet representative at the four-power Berlin air safety center had demanded that certain altitudes in one of the air corridors between Berlin and West Germany be temporarily reserved for Soviet aircraft. He presented a similar demand the next day. Allied authorities rejected the demands and continued their flights as usual. Although the demands were repeated during the next few days, no incident occurred until the 14th when Soviet fighters flew close to several Allied planes but apparently did not actually "buzz" them.

The following day, however, February 15, 1962, MIG's deliberately harassed one British, one French, and three U.S. transports. The fighters, said an Allied official in Berlin, "flew recklessly close to our planes" and "definitely harassed our aircraft by doing acrobatics in the air and cutting up in formation to the Allied transports." The same day the French, British, and U.S. embassies in Moscow presented identical notes protesting the less serious incidents of the day before: "By their actions on Feb. 14, the Soviet Union is running the gravest risks. . . . United States [British] [French] aircraft will continue to fly in the corridors as necessary and in accordance with established procedures. The United States [British] [French] government will take the necessary steps to insure the safety of such flights and will hold the Soviet Government responsible for the consequences of any incidents which might occur."[3]

From Washington, also on the 15th, Max Frankel wrote of

officials indicating "that fighter aircraft had been alerted to come to the aid of any Allied plane in trouble. Regular fighter escort of civilian craft may be ordered if the Russians do not promptly end the harassment. . . . Officials here said increased Soviet pressure would inevitably lead to further action, including counter-harassment of vulnerable Communist traffic in other parts of the world and economic sanctions."

A two-day lull followed. But on the 18th the Soviet representative at the Berlin air safety center again attempted to reserve one of the corridors for the exclusive use of Soviet aircraft. On the 20th Soviet planes resumed flights in the corridors but only after notice had been posted in advance according to the safety-center procedures. No new incidents occurred during the remainder of the month.

In the meantime Khrushchev had opened a campaign for a new summit meeting. In a message delivered to President Kennedy on February 11, he proposed that the eighteen heads of government personally open a disarmament conference scheduled to meet at Geneva on March 14. Two days later the President politely declined the invitation but left the door open for a summit meeting at a later date. The Soviet chargé in Washington delivered a second message on the 22nd—an argumentative and propaganda laden document of twenty pages repeating the suggestion. Two days later Mr. Kennedy again rejected the proposal.

In the issue of the 20th, *Izvestia* had expressed dissatisfaction with the exploratory talks on Berlin which Foreign Minister Gromyko and U.S. Ambassador Thompson had been carrying on since early in January. "It has been indicated to Mr. Thompson," reported Seymour Topping from Moscow on February 21, "that the talks may be broken off soon unless there is a change in the Western position. The implication is that Moscow will sign a separate peace treaty with East Germany and turn control of the land and air access routes to West Berlin over to the East German Communist regime." Ulbricht conferred with Khrushchev in Moscow on the 26th and 27th. The two discussed Berlin and a German peace treaty, and the Soviet Premier promised additional credits to brace the shaky East-zone economy for any new crisis. And at Leipzig on March 5, Anastas I. Mikoyan, First Deputy Soviet Premier, signed a trade and aid agreement involving a credit of one and three tenths billion marks and some two billion marks in trade. Finally, on March 11, *Izvestia* hinted at a new deadline for a German peace treaty.

At approximately the same time Khrushchev was attempting one last slice at West Berlin's air communications. Soviet fighters were rumored to have "buzzed" a British and an American transport early in March, and on the 9th Soviet planes began dropping "chaff," strips of metal foil, in the air corridors to confuse Allied radar operators. At Geneva two days later, Secretary of State Rusk and Lord Home, the British Foreign Secretary, protested to Gromyko. "We told him we did not like it at all," Mr. Rusk informed reporters. But on the 12th the Washington bureau of the *New York Times* reported a somewhat stronger reaction:

The United States Air Force is prepared to fly fighter escorts for commercial planes in the three air corridors between West Germany and West Berlin if Soviet harassment continued, officials here said tonight. Two weeks ago, when the Soviet Union tried to pre-empt altitudes at which Western commercial flights would be made, Gen. Lauris Norstad, commander in chief of the North

5 BACK TO THE OLD SALAMI SLICER

Atlantic Treaty Organization forces, placed some United States fighter aircraft on a five-minute alert in case they were needed to safeguard the Western planes. Officials said General Norstad had authority to take any action he deemed necessary to preserve flight safety.

Yes, Nikita Sergeyevich, there may be a Santa Claus. But he doesn't necessarily live in the White House after all! And with his extensive experience in drawing logical conclusions, the Soviet Premier soon arrived at this one. Soviet planes again dropped foil in the air corridors on the 13th, but the report from Washington quoted above appeared in the *New York Times* the same day and this particular maneuver was not repeated. But Khrushchev could not order an immediate stand-down without losing face, and Soviet flights in the corridors continued, even increased, during the following two weeks. In conversations with Western visitors, officials of the Soviet Embassy in East Berlin stressed the right of Soviet transports to fly in the corridors and declared that they would continue to do so until the signing of a German peace treaty.

In a Kremlin speech of March 16, Nikita Sergeyevich rattled his rockets quite ferociously (to cover up for the coming stand-down?) but adopted a surprisingly mild tone on Berlin. And in talks with Secretary of State Rusk at Geneva toward the end of the month, Foreign Minister Gromyko assumed a somewhat milder attitude on the Berlin problem. In private conversations, Soviet officials sought to conceal the retreat by adopting a "sour grapes" attitude regarding West Berlin, hinting that they weren't interested in the city after all. "In the West," wrote Seymour Topping from Moscow on April 2, "there is a tendency to regard the future of West Berlin as the pivotal question . . . This is not the case here with regard to both public opinion and to the apparent attitudes of the Soviet leaders. Soviet officials tacitly admit that West Berlin is viewed primarily as a sensitive Western nerve to be pressed at those moments when the Western powers seem to be losing interest in negotiating about Germany as a whole."

The last (for the time being at least) Soviet aircraft flew in the air corridors on March 29, 1962. At the same time harassment of Allied military convoys on the autobahn ceased; some had been held up for two hours or more. On March 10 East-zone police had fired on and seriously wounded the driver of an auto carrying a member of the British liaison mission with the Soviet headquarters in East Germany. Ten days later police fired on a car of the American liaison mission. The U.S. Army retaliated by suspending the activities of its mission and forbidding members of a similar Soviet mission in West Germany to leave their quarters without an American escort. The Soviet forces retaliated in turn by placing a guard around the quarters of the American mission and forbidding travel without specific permission. General Bruce C. Clarke, the retiring U.S. Army commander in Europe, visited Marshal Konev on April 5 and was accorded a friendly reception which featured large quantities of caviar and vodka. A joint communiqué released at the end of the visit said that future operations of the two missions would be in accordance with the original 1947 agreement. The next day guards on both missions were withdrawn.

In Washington on April 10, it was disclosed that General Clay would resign his Berlin post within a few weeks. Nine days later TASS announced the relief of Marshal Konev as Soviet commander in East Germany. The same day Khrushchev addressed a Komsomol congress: "We are keeping the Western hotheads at bay," he declared, "by the strength and might of the Soviet armed forces and the might of all the Socialist camp." And reporting to the Supreme Soviet on April 24, Foreign Minister Gromyko adopted a restrained tone but admitted that talks at Geneva had resulted in "some glimpses of hope that agreement is possible." At about this time Colonel Solovyev, the Soviet commander in East Berlin, was promoted to major general, a promotion putting him on the same level as his Western opposite numbers. Finally, on May 15, the East-zone news agency announced the release of some East German troops from active duty.

Although quite handy with proverbs, Nikita Sergeyevich never did quote the one that applies to Washington's handling of the 1960–62 Berlin crisis—the one about grasping nettles!

6

Again Berlin—as Bogy
(July–October 18, 1962)

IN MARCH 1962 Khrushchev seems to have concluded that he had gone as far as he dared with respect to West Berlin. The city could scarcely be taken by a direct attack without provoking a major war, any further action against air communications would involve shooting down Allied planes, and a surface blockade, which had failed once before, might invite serious retaliation.

But Berlin, although certainly a prize in its own right, was important mainly as a political weather-vane. By February 1948, after Munich, six years of German occupation, and the imposition of Communist governments throughout Eastern Europe, too many Czechs had decided they could expect no support from the West and should seek the best terms possible from their most powerful neighbor, i.e. join the Czechoslovak Communist Party. And the majority who had not joined were too fearful and disheartened to oppose the Communist coup in February. Had the United States abandoned Berlin as a result of Stalin's subsequent blockade, many Frenchmen and Italians would also have decided to take out political insurance by joining the Communists, and Europe today might consist of Soviet satellites as far as the Pyrenees. (The other side of the coin bears a similar imprint: Moscow cannot agree to meaningful unification of Germany without abandoning the East-zone regime. Should this occur, Communist officials in some other satellites, police especially, fearful that they too might find themselves without Soviet protection, would hesitate to crack down on expressions of discontent. Emboldened by such leniency, opposition could snowball and soon culminate in several repetitions of the Hungarian uprising or the collapse of the Party in Czechoslovakia. It may be significant that the Hungarian revolt followed the Soviet withdrawal from neighboring Austria by little more than a year.)

But weather vanes might be found outside Europe. Were Khrushchev able to demonstrate American unwillingness to oppose Soviet encroachments elsewhere—in Cuba for example—the result would be comparable to a Western surrender on Berlin. Prime Minister Macmillan gave one of the best and most succinct explanations of the Cuban crisis in the House of Commons on October 25, 1962: "In view of the President's pledge that the United States would take measures to oppose the creation of offensive military power in Cuba, the Russian action, contrary to their categorical assurances, in developing this power can be only regarded as a deliberate adventure designed to test the ability and determination of the United States. The President, no doubt, formed the view, and, in my judgment, rightly, that to have accepted this would throw doubt on America's pledges in all parts of the world and expose the entire free world to a new series of perils."[1]

And while the Soviet Union would clearly be the aggressor in any action against Berlin, Khrushchev felt the United States would have to assume this role in opposing any military build-up in Cuba. The prospect of cold-bloodedly attacking a weak neighbor could be expected to cloud the judgment (?) and paralyze the will of those American "liberals" who display such touching faith in the United Nations, World Public Opinion, Santa Claus (presumably), etc. On September 9 Robert Frost returned from a brief visit to the U.S.S.R. "Khrushchev said he feared for us modern liberals," the poet told reporters. "He said we were too liberal to fight. I suppose he thought we'd stand there for the next hundred years saying, 'On the one hand—but on the other hand.'"[2] (Mr. Frost may have misunderstood the remark. Or was he exercising some justified poetic license?)

During the first half of 1962, signs of strain were apparent in Moscow's relations with Havana. Castro had denounced and purged a veteran Cuban Communist who attempted to capture his revolutionary organization, and the Soviet Government had abruptly recalled its ambassador and appointed the third-ranking member of the Havana embassy in his place. As late as August 18, Tad Szulc of the *New York Times* compared Cuba to a millstone about Khrushchev's neck. "It poses for him the immense dilemma that while on the one hand the collapsing Cuban economy is an increasing and perhaps ultimately useless drain on the Soviet resources as well as an embarrassing demonstration of the operations of a new Communist society, on the other hand Moscow cannot afford politically to jettison the Castro regime."

On July 2, 1962, however, Raul Castro, Minister of the Cuban Armed Forces and brother of Premier Fidel Castro, had arrived in Moscow with a party of Cuban officers for a seventeen-day visit. Soviet Defense Minister Malinovsky welcomed the party at the airport. The next day Khrushchev received them in the Kremlin, with Malinovsky again present. During the next few days the officers visited military installations, were featured in the Soviet press, and on the 8th attended a state dinner in the Kremlin. No further reports of their activities appeared, and Western correspondents in Moscow assumed they were engaged in talks with Soviet officers. Evidently the two parties soon reached an agreement on the details of a major Soviet build-up in Cuba. It may have started even before the visitors left Moscow; eight Soviet-bloc ships, which must have left Russian ports at least ten days earlier, arrived in Cuba between July 26 and August 8. Most of them were unloaded at night with strict security precautions, an indication that the cargoes consisted largely of military equipment.

Once Khrushchev had decided on the Cuban venture, Berlin again became important—not as a prize in itself but as an instrument for paralyzing U.S. policy elsewhere. As we have seen, he apparently initiated the Berlin "crisis" in November 1958 to deter Britain and the United States from any further vigorous action in the Middle East.

A political lull had followed the Soviet stand-down in March 1962, and the "crisis" had grown lukewarm, almost cold. But on July 10, eight days after Raul Castro's arrival in Moscow, the Soviet Premier addressed a Communist-front peace congress in the Kremlin and added fresh charcoal to the Berlin samovar. His government, said Khrushchev, would accept replacement of the "occupation forces" in West Berlin by neutral or United Nations troops: "As no agreement has been reached on this matter, we suggest that the troops to be stationed in West Berlin should be those of Norway and Denmark or of Belgium and the Netherlands, as well as those of Poland and Czechoslovakia. Needless to say that those troops should be under the United Nations flag, and should not represent either of the existing military alignments."[3]

Before the day was out, the State Department had declared the proposal unacceptable. It was one of several advanced and rejected earlier in private talks, officials explained. The Soviet Premier, they intimated, for propaganda reasons was making what he knew to be an unacceptable offer. Two days later Moscow replied in a TASS statement released with some fanfare: Correspondents summoned to the Foreign Ministry received an advance text at 7:30 P.M., and the statement was read over the Moscow radio and television several hours later. From the State Department's attitude, said TASS,

it follows that the United States Government insists on its former unrealistic position on the question of the troops of the three powers in West Berlin and on the necessity of keeping West Berlin as a military base of NATO. Well, if such is the position of the United States, then the Soviet Union together with other peace-loving states will have to solve the question of signing a German peace treaty and settling on its basis the situation in West Berlin without the participation of the Western powers. . . .

A new situation will be created . . . after a peace treaty with the G.D.R. is signed. . . . the sovereignty of the German Democratic Republic will be fully restored, including its control over the ways of communications running through its territory and its air space. As repeatedly stated, after the signing of a peace treaty West Berlin will be regarded by the signatories of the treaty as a free, demilitarized city with all consequences this entails.[4]

In an interview with a group of visiting American newspaper editors in Moscow on the 13th, Khrushchev devoted more than half an hour to Berlin which he termed the "key issue in the present international situation." At the same time he assured the visitors that his government would sign a separate treaty only after making every effort to convince the Western powers of the justice of the Soviet position. "I will not set a time limit," said the Premier. But the same day the Soviet Embassy in Bonn disclosed that Ambassador Smirnov had been ordered home for consultations and would fly to Moscow the next day.

Max Frankel commented on the situation in a dispatch from Washington, also on the 13th: Without any especially provocative action in Berlin and without saying anything really new, "Moscow has managed to create a mood of new danger and threat without running the diplomatic risk of threatening anything. Through the energetic revival of the magic phrase 'peace treaty,' the West's newspapers have done most of the Russians' work for them."

As early as July 16, President Kennedy had asked Anatoly F. Dobrynin, the new Soviet Ambassador to Washington, to call at the White House. The call took place the next day, and Pierre Salinger, the White House press secretary, sought to give the impression that it was not unusual. But Mikhail A. Menshikov, Ambassador Dobrynin's predecessor, had called alone at the White House only once, and then merely to deliver Khrushchev's agreement to the Vienna summit meeting. According to other officials, reported E. W. Kenworthy of the *New York Times*, Secretary of State Rusk had warned the ambassador a few days earlier that the Allied forces in Berlin were not negotiable. "Lest there be any doubt that the United States was adamant on this point, it was decided that President Kennedy himself should state it forcefully to Mr. Dobrynin."

In Geneva for the signing of a multilateral agreement on Laos, Mr. Rusk spoke with the Soviet Foreign Minister on July 21, 22, and 24. Sydney Gruson covered the meeting: "Mr. Gromyko," he wrote on the 22nd, "is reported to have told Secretary of State Rusk yesterday that the peace treaty 'with all its consequences' would be signed if there was no Berlin agreement." And after the last conversation on the 24th: "It is assumed that Mr. Gromyko had repeated what he has been saying on every opportunity since he got here: that the Russians would go ahead with the peace treaty if no Berlin agreement is reached." President Kennedy also referred to the matter during his news conference on July 23: "We have made no progress recently on the Berlin settlement. . . . I cannot report progress . . . We hope that an accord can be reached. We continue to try to reach one. But we've not made progress recently."[5]

Of course mere hints and statements could scarcely keep the "crisis" warm for very long—much less raise it to a boil. Hence on the morning of July 17 a Soviet fighter had passed within a few hundred feet of a Pan American airliner flying from Berlin to West Germany. Twenty-five minutes later, a Soviet jet made a deliberate pass 300 to 400 feet in front of a U.S. Federal Aviation Agency transport en route to Berlin. The next day the East-zone press office announced the arrest of fifteen persons on the autobahn, all allegedly on criminal charges. (During the first half of 1962, Communist police were believed to have arrested some 140 West Germans and West Berliners on the autobahn. Most were soon released, however.)

Over Berlin during the morning of the 23rd, two Soviet fighters made a pass at a U.S. Air Force transport at a distance of seventy to eighty feet. That afternoon an MIG-17 flew wing tip to wing tip for seven minutes with a civilian charter plane en route to Berlin. The Russian pilot was so close, said a hostess, "we could see the freckles on his face." American authorities in Berlin believed the buzzing formed part of a deliberate pattern of harassment. "It no longer appears to be a question of isolated incidents," said one official.

Although Soviet jets flew in the air corridors on the 24th without the advance notice required by four-power safety regulations, no incidents occurred. A fighter flew close to a U.S. Air Force courier plane on the 26th, however, and on July 31 a Soviet representative at the Berlin Air Safety Center protested the routine flight of a U.S. Army helicopter over East Berlin the day before. (The agreements establishing the air corridors had also provided for flight within a control zone extending twenty miles from the Berlin air-control center.) "Flights over the Eastern sector have produced objections from the Soviets for some time," explained an American spokesman. "In this case the protest at the Berlin Air Safety Center went so far as to include the statement that we would have to take the consequences, which might even include the shooting down of the helicopter." But the next day a U.S. helicopter flew over East Berlin without incident.

Ulbricht and Willi Stoph, acting Premier of the East-zone regime, flew to Russia on August 1, and journalists immediately assumed some connection with the peace treaty. On the 7th Soviet Ambassador Smirnov returned from Moscow where, as other members of the Bonn embassy disclosed, he had "fundamental discussions over the present state of Soviet-German relations." And two days later Willi Stoph published an article in *Isvestia,* the official daily of the Soviet Government: "The events of the last weeks and months show more and more clearly to our population that the conclusion of a peace treaty and the conversion on this basis of West Berlin into a demilitarized free city cannot be posponed any longer."

The next ominous move occurred on August 22 when the Soviet Defense Ministry abolished General Solovyev's East Berlin headquarters and transferred its functions to the Soviet commander in East Germany. The Western commanders in Berlin, said the official announcement, "are trying to take advantage of the existence of the Soviet commandant's office to present unjustified claims to interference of the Western powers in the international affairs of the sovereign and independent German Democratic Republic and its capital." The next day a U.S. Army convoy was delayed for half an hour on the autobahn, and the day after that, the 24th, another convoy was held up for six and a half hours.

In the meantime the Soviet campaign to emphasize the dangers of the Berlin situation received an unexpected impetus for which Khrushchev was only indirectly responsible. In West Berlin at noon on August 13, the first anniversary of the sealing off of the eastern sector of the city, traffic halted for what was supposed to have been three minutes of silence. But instead motorists turned the occasion into a period of horn blowing. More serious disorders during the day involved five to ten thousand young West Berliners; crowds threw stones over the wall at several points and also at several Soviet military vehicles. Twenty-four West Berlin policemen were injured while attempting to maintain order.

Four days later, on August 17, Communist guards shot an eighteen-year-old East Berlin youth, Peter Fechter, as he was attempting to escape over the wall. The guards then left the dying youth to lie on their side of the wall without medical attention for more than an hour. Of course hundreds of similar although not quite so barbarous incidents had occurred in the year since the wall's erection. But the mood of West Berlin had changed radically during the same year; unlike the people of Prague in February 1948, the people of West Berlin in August 1962 believed they would not be abandoned by the West. An action which would merely have added to the sense of fear a year earlier sent a wave of indignation through the city in August 1962.

Since shortly after the end of World War II, the Soviet Army had maintained sentries at a memorial in the British sector near the Brandenburg Gate. After August 1961 the reliefs had proceeded by bus through the Friedrichstrasse crossing point. During most of August 19, 1962, West Berlin police held a rather large crowd some fifty yards back from the crossing point. At 6:00 P.M., however, when the Soviet bus appeared, the crowd broke through the police lines and smashed practically all its windows. But the demonstrators scattered when the driver stepped on the gas, and the bus escaped to the memorial and the protection of barbed wire and British troops. The next evening saw a similar incident; this time two of the Soviet soldiers in the bus were injured. And Soviet officers in an auto sought refuge in the U.S. Army's McNair Barracks after having been chased across West Berlin by angry crowds and were given a military police escort back to the border. Later in the evening a crowd estimated at 5,000 battled 400 policemen in a demonstration near the wall.

According to one subsequent account, worried officials in Washington were urging American authorities in West Berlin to avoid any serious incident. Thus when Soviet officers informed the U.S. mission that they would relieve the memorial guard in armored cars rather than buses, the action was greeted almost with relief. When three Soviet armored cars appeared at the crossing point late in the evening of the 21st, they were quickly given an escort and allowed to proceed. But Allied authorities soon came to regard the Soviet armor as a sort of camel's nose and gingerly began to restrict its use. At the Friedrichstrasse crossing on the afternoon of September 2, an American official read the text of Allied instructions to the Soviet colonel in charge of the relief: After the 3rd, the armored-car convoys would have to enter West Berlin via the Sandkrug Bridge, about a mile from the memorial, or the Brandenburg Gate, only a few hundred feet from it. (The Friedrichstrasse crossing was two miles from the monument.) And during the evening of the 4th, the cars appeared at the Sandkrug Bridge.

Encouraged by this success, Allied authorities in Berlin soon began to hint that they would bar the armor altogether. On September 12 it was disclosed that the Allies had given the Soviet Army three days to revert to the use of buses. A British officer read a statement to this effect on the 13th to the officer in charge of the memorial guards, and the next day the relief appeared at the Sandkrug Bridge in a bus. This was the only encouraging development in Berlin, however, and was certainly not enough to offset Khrushchev's earlier threatening moves.

In the meantime the Soviet Premier had been adding fresh fuel to bring the simmering Berlin "crisis" to a boil. A Soviet statement of September 11 on Cuba had closed with a short section emphasizing the necessity of a German peace treaty: "It is said that it is difficult for the United States to negotiate on the German peace treaty now as elections to the American Congress are due in November. Well, the Soviet Government is prepared to reckon with this, but one cannot link the solution of the question of a German peace treaty all the time to elections in this or that country."[6] At first glance this may have seemed a moderate retreat, yet it also implied that Moscow would press the issue after November 6. As the statement was actually interpreted in Washington, Khrushchev had laid down a new deadline—"crisis by appointment," one reporter called it—and without the risk of having to lift a deadline couched as such. And in a speech in Leipzig three days earlier, Ulbricht had reportedly claimed a definite date had been fixed for signing the treaty, but this remark was deleted in the version published in *Neues Deutschland* on September 13.

Few Western diplomats in Moscow, wrote Seymour Topping from the Soviet capital on September 16, expected any move on Berlin which would create a serious risk of war. "It is felt here," he continued,

that Premier Khrushchev might be tempted to take such a gamble only if the United States intervened militarily in Cuba. . . . These impressions are based on private conversations Premier Khrushchev has held with a succession of visitors in recent weeks at his vacation villas. . . . The substance of these conversations usually leaks and the impact sometimes helps Premier Khrushchev to create an atmosphere he wants for the conduct of his diplomacy. These informal conversations, although they often contain some assertion of a determination to take action, are not binding on the Soviet state in the same way a diplomatic note or Government statement would be.

Two days later the Soviet Premier granted an interview to Raymond Scheyven, a former Belgian Economics Minister. "Without doubt," declared Khrushchev, "we will continue the dialogue with the Americans after the American elections in November . . . But if the Americans persist with their present unrealistic attitude, it is possible that we will turn to the U.N. We will notify the world organization of our intention to sign a peace treaty . . . and we will present the definitions of this treaty."[7]

Interference with West Berlin's communications resumed the next day, September 19, when Soviet officers delayed a U.S. Army convoy for three hours and nineteen minutes on the autobahn. Two days later East German police held up truck traffic on the autobahn for over three hours. The Russians delayed another American convoy for more than two hours on the 24th, and the next day Soviet fighters buzzed a U.S. Air Force transport and an Air France commercial airliner. Finally, on the 26th, a Soviet jet approached a Pan American airliner head-on in a clear sky and missed it by only 150 yards. The civilian plane carried eighty-four passengers and a crew of five.

Returning from a two-day inspection trip to West Germany, Secretary of Defense Robert S. McNamara hurriedly scheduled a press conference on September 28, only hours after his return. The current crisis, said Mr. McNamara, was worse than any since the Korean War. He explained that "Premier Khrushchev's insistence on a peace treaty and possible actions after that would restrict our rights in Berlin make it as critical as it is." The United States, the Defense Secretary warned, would use nuclear weapons if necessary: "It is our policy to utilize whatever weapons are needed to preserve our vital interests. Quite clearly, we consider access to Berlin a vital interest."[8] And the next day E. W. Kenworthy of the *New York Times* quoted a "high State Department official": At this moment "we're on a collision course."

At a luncheon on the 30th, President Kennedy discussed the Berlin situation with Lord Home, the British Foreign Secretary, Secretary Rusk, Under Secretary of State George W. Ball, the British Ambassador, and the U.S. Ambassador to London. The participants reviewed conversations Mr. Rusk and Lord Home had had with Foreign Minister Gromyko at the United Nations, and, according to the joint statement released later, "there was complete agreement on the assessment of the dangers of the Berlin situation and on the continued need for the Western powers to stand firm on their vital interests."

From Washington the same day, James Reston wrote of "the growing conviction here that the Soviet Union will sign a peace treaty with the Communist East German regime, probably in mid-November. . . . There is a greater sense of anxiety in Washington over Berlin than at any time since November, 1958 . . . the State Department has recently received what is described as 'numerous' indications that Moscow intends to take this step shortly after the November Congressional elections."

Rumors of a visit by Khrushchev to the United Nations

also began to receive increasing credence at this time. Responsible sources had made no direct statement about a visit, but "high Soviet officials in Moscow have dropped a number of hints to foreign visitors," reported Max Frankel from Washington on October 5. Mayor Brandt of West Berlin, who left Washington the same day after a week of conversations, considered a visit "probable." He reportedly feared the Soviet Premier would arrive in New York immediately after a new Berlin move, e.g., declaring East Germany sovereign and instituting visas for travel to West Berlin. From Moscow two days later, Seymour Topping reported editorials in the Soviet press which might be interpreted as attempting to brace the public for a new Berlin crisis. Western observers in Moscow, he wrote, felt the Soviet Premier might go to New York primarily "to obtain the support of the nonaligned countries for a separate peace treaty with East Germany." And on the 13th Mr. Topping reported that "Soviet hints with military overtones are being dropped here almost daily about the serious consequences that might result if a Berlin settlement is not achieved soon."

In Washington on the 11th, Max Frankel had written of the President and his advisers making a determined effort to persuade the country and its allies of the danger of an impending crisis over Berlin. In addition to preventing any surprise and keeping Cuba from distracting official and public opinion, talk of a crisis "should prevent miscalculation in Moscow . . . should persuade Premier Khrushchev to continue to tread prudently in Berlin and should enable him and other Communists—if they wish—to urge caution upon more belligerent associates throughout the Soviet bloc." At the United Nations on October 1, Secretary Rusk had warned

Polish Foreign Minister Adam Rapacki of American determination to maintain Western rights in Berlin. Mr. Rusk presumably emphasized this determination in a meeting at the United Nations with Foreign Minister Gromyko on the 6th, a meeting which lasted all afternoon with Berlin forming the sole topic. "According to reliable sources," reported the *New York Times*'s Thomas J. Hamilton from the United Nations on the 14th, "some United States officials fear that a Soviet surprise attack on the Western garrisons in West Berlin might come at any time." In Berlin on the 14th, Mayor Brandt warned of an East German rising should the Communists attempt a military attack on West Berlin. And in a radio and television interview the same day, Presidential assistant McGeorge Bundy said the United States would act alone if necessary, without its allies, to protect West Berlin.

In the meantime, Soviet deliveries to Cuba had increased sharply at the end of July, and on August 24 Roger Hilsman, the State Department's intelligence chief, told reporters that some twenty freighters plus a number of passenger vessels had docked since then. Estimates of the number of Soviet "technicians" ranged from three to five thousand. Most of the cargoes had been unloaded secretly at night by the ships' crews and specially selected members of the Cuban militia.

In a speech on August 27, Senator Homer E. Capehart of Indiana charged that most of the Soviet personnel were combat troops and repeated an earlier demand for an invasion of Cuba: "How long will the President examine the situation as he told his press conference [of August 22] he is doing?" asked the Senator. "Until the hundreds of Russian troops grow into hundreds of thousands? Until the little Cuban military force grows into a big Russian force?"[9]

In another Presidential news conference on August 29, a reporter asked Mr. Kennedy to comment on Senator Capehart's speech. "We have no evidence of troops," said the President. "And unless they—I know that this matter is of great concern to Americans and many others. The United States has obligations all around the world, including West Berlin and other areas which are very sensitive, and therefore I think that in considering what appropriate action we should take we have to consider the totality of our obligations and also the responsibilities which we bear in so many different parts of the world. . . . I'm not for invading Cuba at this time. No, I don't have any, the words do not have some secondary meaning. I think it would be a mistake to invade Cuba."[10] Khrushchev must have rubbed his hands in glee when he read the translation of this remark. The Berlin "crisis" was working exactly as planned.[11]

Although operating in a different theater, the Soviet Premier continued to use the same salami tactics he had used a few months earlier in the real Berlin crisis. The shipments in July and August represented the first slice—which had not aroused Washington. The second was to unveil some of the arms already delivered and see if this would provoke any dangerous American reaction.

Reports of antiaircraft rockets in Cuba had begun to reach Washington as early as mid-August. A few were already set up in firing positions by August 29. And a short announcement of Soviet arms aid to Cuba was inserted in a communiqué released in Moscow on September 2. (Ernesto Guevara, the Cuban Minister of Industry, and Emilio Aragones Navarro, head of the Cuban militia, had arrived in Moscow on August 27 to discuss economic aid. The communiqué, issued at the end of their visit, dealt mainly with purely economic questions.) Because of the "threats of aggressive imperialist quarters," ran the announcement, the Cuban Government had appealed to the Soviet Union for armaments and "technical specialists for training Cuban servicemen." The Soviet Government had considered the appeal, "and agreement was reached on this question. As long as the above mentioned quarters continue threatening Cuba, the Cuban Republic has every justification for taking necessary measures to insure its security and safeguard its sovereignty and independence, while all Cuba's true friends have every right to respond to this legitimate request."[12]

The White House replied on September 4 with a statement by President Kennedy: "Information has reached this Government in the last four days from a variety of sources which establishes without doubt that the Soviets have provided the Cuban Government with a number of anti-aircraft defensive missiles . . . There is no evidence of any organized combat force in Cuba from any Soviet bloc country; of military bases provided to Russia . . . of the presence of offensive ground-to-ground missiles . . . Were it to be otherwise the gravest issues would arise." And the President's statement gave fresh evidence of the influence of the Berlin "crisis": The Cuban problem formed a "part of the world-wide challenge posed by Communist threats to the peace. It must be dealt with as a part of that larger issue."[13]

Although Kennedy placed the number of Soviet-bloc military personnel in Cuba at 3,500, he denied evidence of "any organized combat force" of Soviet troops. But reports in the next few days from refugees, diplomats in Havana, and Cuban underground organizations indicated the presence of

4,000 Soviet soldiers organized in separate units with their own trucks, supplies, and arms. These were in addition to the Soviet instructors attached to Cuban units. On September 7, the Republican leaders in Congress, Senator Everett M. Dirksen and Representative Charles A. Halleck, proposed a resolution authorizing the President to use troops in Cuba if necessary. Five days later a Cuban Air Force lieutenant, who had defected and landed at Key West on September 4, stated that 200 Soviet jet fighters were in Cuba, including some modern MIG-19's.

In Moscow at noon on September 11, correspondents were called to the Foreign Ministry to hear a long, rambling statement. The same afternoon the home service of the Moscow radio devoted thirty-five minutes to reading the text. Apparently the Soviet Government sought primarily to reassure both domestic and foreign opinion on the Cuban situation.[14] Referring to the military aid, the statement declared "that the number of Soviet military specialists sent to Cuba can in no way be compared to the number of workers in agriculture and industry sent there. The armaments and military equipment sent to Cuba are designed exclusively for defensive purposes."

The Soviet Government denied any "need for the Soviet Union to shift its weapons for the repulsion of aggression, for a retaliatory blow, to any other country, for instance Cuba. Our nuclear weapons are so powerful in their explosive force and the Soviet Union has so powerful rockets to carry these nuclear warheads that there is no need to search for sites for them beyond the boundaries of the Soviet Union."

The statement also referred to an announcement made four days earlier regarding "the discharge into reserve of the service men who have completed their term. Trained soldiers are being released from the armed forces of the U.S.S.R. and recruits are being called up to replenish the units. This alone is a clear enough indication of our peaceful intentions." (Because of the Berlin crisis of the previous year, conscripts had been retained on active duty beyond their normal period of service.)

Moscow also attempted to justify the Cuban build-up by pointing to American bases and forces abroad:

The whole world knows that the United States of America has ringed the Soviet Union and other Socialist countries with bases. . . . these armaments, stationed along the frontiers of the Soviet Union—in Turkey, Iran, Greece, Italy, Britain, Holland, Pakistan and other countries belonging to the military blocs of NATO, CENTO and SEATO—are said to be there lawfully, by right. They consider this their right! But to others the U.S. does not permit this even for defense, and when measures are nevertheless taken to strengthen the defenses of this or that country the U.S. raises an outcry and declares that an attack, if you please, is being prepared against them.

This particular argument recalls Hitler's bitter complaints in 1939 against Britain's "encirclement" policy.

Khrushchev apparently meant the statement primarily as a soothing gesture. But it also contained a warning, "that one cannot now attack Cuba and expect that the aggressor will be free from punishment for this attack. If this attack is made, this will be the beginning of the unleashing of war." This and related passages may have been included as a sort of prod—very much as the dentist prods the gum several minutes after injecting the Novocain and asks, "Do you feel this?"

"No, not yet," replied President Kennedy in effect two days later. He began his press conference of September 13 with a lengthy statement. Should Cuba ever "become an offensive military base of significant capacity for the Soviet Union," he warned, "then this country will do whatever must be done to protect its own security and that of its allies." The first subsequent question was "at what point do you determine that the build-up in Cuba has lost its defensive guise to become offensive? Would it take an overt act?" In reply the President cited the statement just made and the one of September 4. "I've made it quite clear, particularly in last week's statement when we talked about the presence of offensive military missile capacity or development of military bases."[15]

"Ok, young fellow," Nikita Sergeyevich must have thought as he read this exchange in translation, "you want a military base—you'll get a military base. Let's see what you do about it!" Rumors of a naval base planned by the Castro regime began to leak out of Cuba as early as September 18, and in a television address on the 25th Fidel Castro announced the signing of a Cuban-Soviet fishing treaty and agreement on the construction of a fishing port to service Soviet trawlers. Both countries were to share the costs of the project which was to be built by Cuban labor with Cuban materials.

Earlier in Washington, Gromyko had conferred for three hours with Secretary of State Rusk. As he left the meeting, reporters asked if the "proposed base" had been mentioned. "I would not use such terms as base," replied the Soviet Foreign Minister. But on the 26th TASS reported that the port would accommodate up to 130 vessels. An account in *Izvestia* on the 27th reduced this figure to fifteen or twenty trawlers.) According to TASS, the Soviet Union would provide assistance in building "wharves, freezers, storage warehouses, repair shops with a floating dock, oil storage facilities, a radio station and other auxiliary installations." And from Washington on the 26th, Jack Raymond of the *New York Times* reported concern at the Department of Defense "that such a port could be turned to military purposes, such as supporting Soviet submarines or trawlers observing United States military and missile operations in the Caribbean area."

Khrushchev must have found Washington's reaction, or rather lack of reaction, to this move quite encouraging. On October 4, administration officials disclosed a four-point program to reduce Soviet shipments to Cuba:[16] (1) The United States would refuse to ship government-owned cargo in the ships of a line or owner engaging in Soviet bloc-Cuba trade. (2) Ships delivering Communist supplies to Cuba could not take on freight in U.S. ports for the return trip. (3) Ships flying the American flag or owned in the United States would not be allowed to trade with Cuba. In view of the large number of idle tramp steamers, these measures could scarcely have any serious effect on Soviet-Cuban trade, but the fourth point was obviously meaningless: (4) American ports would be closed to all the ships of a country allowing vessels under its flag to carry military equipment to Cuba. Soviet ships had carried all the military cargoes, and the Soviet flag was practically never seen in American ports. And officials also emphasized that, for the time being, the restrictions would not apply to shipments from non-Communist countries. In other words, the plan gave every appearance of having been designed mainly to appease American public opinion. It may very well be that Khrushchev gave the final OK for missile sites in Cuba only after learning of these weak measures.[17]

The Cuban extraction, which was to expose Uncle Sam as toothless and feeble, was already under way when Nikita Sergeyevich and his Foreign Minister administered the final shots of Novocain and brandished Berlin menacingly for the last time. Khrushchev called the new U.S. Ambassador, Foy D. Kohler, to the Kremlin on October 16. The Soviet Premier was genial and warmly reassuring about Cuba. He expressed regret at any political trouble the news of the Soviet fishing port might have caused Mr. Kennedy. The announcement, said Khrushchev, had been made without his knowledge while he was in the Crimea. The Soviet program in Cuba was purely defensive, and he certainly had not intended to embarrass the President on the eve of the Congressional elections. According to a report from Moscow (Seymour Topping) the same day, the Soviet Premier also "emphasized" his government's intention to seriously press the Berlin issue after the American elections.

Two days later in Washington, Gromyko met with President Kennedy for two hours and fifteen minutes, at the Foreign Minister's request. The first part of the talk was devoted to Berlin: Gromyko assured the President that his government would do nothing about Berlin before the elections unless forced to do so. Read "unless the United States attacked Cuba"? But should there be no agreement after that date, the Soviet Foreign Minister continued, Moscow would be compelled to sign a peace treaty and take all the necessary steps proceeding from it. Gromyko also denied that Cuba constituted a threat to the United States. Soviet assistance was purely for economic and defense purposes, he said, and Soviet instructors had given no training in the use of offensive weapons.[18]

7

"And It Soft As Silk Remains"
(September–December 1962)

AN AMERICAN U-2 had flown over most of Cuba on August 29 and another on September 5. The two flights had yielded excellent photographic coverage of the central and western parts of the island. Three more flights, of September 17 and 26 and October 5, covered eastern Cuba, and one of September 29 photographed the Isle of Pines and the Bay of Pigs. In the meantime, however, a Nationalist U-2 had been downed over mainland China on September 9, and members of the U.S. intelligence community were reluctant to send an aircraft directly over western Cuba where the sites for antiaircraft rockets were most advanced and most numerous. As Roger Hilsman later recalled, "no one wanted to risk a man's life needlessly or to raise an international political storm that might restrict the flights in some way and thus limit our best source of intelligence."

On October 4, however, a special intelligence meeting convened to consider flights over the western end of the island, which had not been covered for a month, and one was approved on the 9th. Delayed by predictions of cloudy

125

skies, the U-2 finally took off and completed its mission without incident on October 14. But some of the pictures it took were as startling as the flight had been uneventful. They showed the radar vans, fuel trucks, missile trailers, and launchers of a medium-range Soviet missile battalion.[1]

At this point a question arises: Since the Russians were surely aware of the earlier reconnaissance activities, why had they proceeded so openly? They could easily have erected the smaller medium-range and built the sites for the larger intermediate-range missiles in wooded areas or in areas disguised as tent camps or cantonments. But we must remember, first, that the missiles were in Cuba mainly for their psychological effect—to demonstrate to the world American unwillingness or inability to act. Had the United States not released the aerial photos, TASS would have published close-range pictures a few weeks later. And, second, to have unveiled a large number of missiles at one time would have been contrary to Khrushchev's still cautious step-by-step tactics; it would have meant a dangerously thick slice off the salami. (The intermediate-range missiles, for example, apparently had not yet arrived in Cuba when the medium-range missiles were discovered.)

Several accounts of the crisis also dwell on the delay in setting up the antiaircraft rockets. If they were supposed to mask the installation of the surface-to-surface missiles, they should have been in place and operational several weeks earlier than they actually were. But they may have been merely part of the overall build-up, on a par with the tanks, artillery, and jet fighters. At the same time Khrushchev may have hoped their presence alone would discourage U.S. reconnaissance flights over the crucial areas—which actually happened

—and later deter the Americans from attempting pin-point bombing of the missile sites.

The otherwise inexplicable lack of concealment is the most convincing evidence that Khrushchev's aims were primarily political rather than military. The Soviet regime can hardly have feared an unprovoked nuclear attack by the United States. The U.S. Air Force was able to mount one during most of the 1950's when tensions were much worse and the United States had comparatively little fear of retaliation. And Soviet missiles in Cuba in 1962 would scarcely have deterred an American first-strike. If U.S. target-intelligence could locate missile sites dispersed over the wide expanses of the Soviet Union, how much simpler to hit those concentrated on a relatively small island.

From a purely military point of view, only a surprise attack on the United States would have justified the shipment of Soviet missiles to Cuba. In this case, elementary logic demanded that their presence be kept secret until the moment of firing. Otherwise the U.S. Strategic Air Command could disperse its bombers to auxiliary fields and put more of them on airborne alert and thus increase the risk of an unacceptable retaliatory blow against the Soviet Union.

By the evening of October 15, the high-altitude photos had been developed and examined, and at 8:30 P.M. a C.I.A. official telephoned the news to McGeorge Bundy, the President's special assistant. General Maxwell D. Taylor, Chairman of the Joint Chiefs of Staff, Secretary of State Rusk, and a number of other officials were informed the same evening.

At about 8:45 the next morning, Mr. Bundy brought the pictures and a report prepared during the night to the President's bedroom. Kennedy, still in pajamas and robe, immediately began naming the persons to be called in. Among the chief figures in the discussion and planning of the following days were General Taylor, Mr. Bundy, Secretary Rusk, Secretary of Defense McNamara, Treasury Secretary Douglas Dillon, Attorney General Robert Kennedy, C.I.A. Director John McCone, and Theodore Sorensen, the President's speech writer. Dean Acheson and Robert Lovett, Secretaries of State and Defense respectively under President Truman, and John J. McCloy, former U.S. High Commissioner in Germany, were also called in for advice.

Acceptance of the Soviet move was quickly ruled out. Three other possibilities remained: invasion, bombing of the missile sites, or a blockade of Cuba. The advisory group soon abandoned the idea of an invasion; surprise would be impossible, and it would take too long to prepare. Later photographs had shown work on launching sites for intermediate-range missiles, and it was estimated the first would be ready by November 1, a second two weeks later, and a third by December 1. Although bombing had been seriously considered, by the 19th opinion generally favored a blockade—which would not preclude air action or even an invasion later. The next afternoon President Kennedy tentatively approved a blockade, with the final OK to be given the following day.

In the meantime extensive military measures had been ordered, some as early as October 16. Crews of the Strategic Air Command's intercontinental missiles worked more than seventy hours per week during the crisis; presumably the missiles were kept fueled and ready for launching.

On the morning of the 19th, orders went out alerting the 1st Marine Division at Camp Pendleton, California, and the 2nd at Camp LeJeune, North Carolina. Between October 21 and 23, the Military Air Transport Command flew in some 7,000 Marines, many by jet transport, to reinforce the garrison at the U.S. Naval Base at Guantanamo Bay, Cuba. The 1st Armored Division at Fort Hood, Texas, was alerted on the 21st, and the next day elements of the division began moving via rail and plane to Fort Stewart in southeastern Georgia. Four other Army divisions were also alerted during the crisis, and antiaircraft units were flown to Florida from as far as the Northwest.

The Strategic Air Command began extensive airborne alerts on the 22nd; many of its B-52's were kept in the air for twenty-four hours—with a fresh crew and plane airborne before one already in the air was allowed to land. Altogether during the crisis, S.A.C. crews flew 2,088 sorties, logged 48,532 hours and 20,022,000 miles, and carried out 4,076 aerial refuelings. Thirty-six Navy, Marine Corps, and Air Force pilots later received the Distinguished Flying Cross for reconnaissance flights over and near Cuba during the crisis. To enforce the blockade, the Navy eventually deployed 180 ships, including eight aircraft carriers, one of them the nuclear powered *Enterprise*.

At 11:00 A.M. on Sunday, October 21, certain key officials with specific information the President had requested met in the White House, and Mr. Kennedy gave final approval of the blockade about an hour later. The full National Security Council met formally at 2:30 that afternoon. The President met once more with his top advisers at 9:00 the next morning, the 22nd, and at the same time some twenty Congressional leaders of both parties were summoned back to Washington. At noon White House press secretary Salinger announced that the President would make a very important radio and television address at 7:00 that evening. The National Security Council met again at 3:00 P.M., and a Cabinet meeting followed. The President and Secretary Rusk briefed Congressional leaders at 5:00, and Soviet Ambassador Dobrynin received the news an hour later in Mr. Rusk's office. Finally, at 7:00 P.M., Eastern daylight time, October 22, 1962, the President went on the air.

"Within the past week," said Mr. Kennedy, "unmistakable evidence has established the fact that a series of offensive missile sites is now in preparation [in Cuba] . . . This urgent transformation of Cuba into an important strategic base by the presence of these large long-range and clearly offensive weapons of sudden mass destruction constitutes an explicit threat to the peace and security of all the Americas." It is, he continued, "a deliberately provocative and unjustified change in the status quo which cannot be accepted by this country if our courage and our commitments are ever to be trusted again, by either friend or foe."

To counter this move, the President announced that "a strict quarantine on all offensive military equipment under shipment to Cuba is being initiated. All ships of any kind bound for Cuba from whatever nation or port will, where they are found to contain cargoes of offensive weapons, be turned back. This quarantine will be extended if needed to other types of cargo and carriers. . . . Should these offensive military preparations continue, thus increasing the threat to the hemisphere, further action will be justified."

The term "quarantine" may have been a euphemism, but Mr. Kennedy minced no words in a subsequent passage declaring "the policy of this nation to regard any nuclear missile launched from Cuba against any nation in the Western Hemisphere as an attack by the Soviet Union on the United

States requiring a full retaliatory response upon the Soviet Union."[2]

But the blockade did not follow immediately; although prepared to act alone, the administration preferred Latin-American approval for its measures. The Council of the Organization of American States met at 9:00 the next morning in Washington. Late that afternoon, according to the provisions of the 1947 Inter-American Treaty of Reciprocal Assistance (Rio Treaty), nineteen delegates (the Uruguayan representative was unable to contact his government and abstained) resolved: "1. To call for the immediate dismantling and withdrawal from Cuba of all missiles and other weapons with any offensive capability; 2. To recommend that the member states . . . take all measures, individually and collectively including the use of armed force, which they may deem necessary to ensure that the Government of Cuba cannot continue to receive from the Sino-Soviet powers military material and related supplies which may threaten the peace and security of the continent and to prevent the missiles in Cuba with offensive capability from ever becoming an active threat to the peace and security of the continent."[3] Immediately after this resolution, President Kennedy signed the proclamation of a blockade, to be effective at 10:00 A.M., eastern daylight time, the next day, October 24.

The Kremlin remained silent for thirteen hours following the President's speech. Finally, at 3:00 P.M., Moscow time, on the 23rd, Ambassador Kohler was summoned to the Soviet Foreign Ministry and handed an official statement. Half an hour later, carefully avoiding any mention of missiles in Cuba, the Moscow radio broadcast a short summary of the speech and the complete text of the Soviet statement.

The statement itself seems to have been merely for the record; although rather vituperative, it contained nothing that had not been said before: Moscow accused the United States of attempting to stifle Cuban sovereignty, of being prepared to "attack ships of other states on the high seas—i.e., to engage in piracy," and of "recklessly playing with fire." But in case of aggression "the Soviet Union would strike a most powerful retaliatory blow." (Aggression against Cuba was implied but nowhere specifically stated.) The statement contained the usual soothing expression: "As to the Soviet Union's assistance to Cuba, it is aimed solely at enhancing Cuba's defense potential." A sentence near the end summed up the general tone and substance: "The establishment of an actual blockade of the Cuban shores by the United States is a provocative move, an unheard-of violation of international law, a challenge to all peace-loving nations."[4]

The blockade became effective at 10:00 on the morning of the 24th; although the Soviet Foreign Ministry refused to accept a copy of the proclamation and a covering note, within a few hours twelve Soviet ships en route to Cuba had changed course to avoid an encounter with the U.S. Navy. The same day, "competent sources" in Warsaw indicated Polish ships would submit to search under protest. Although a demonstration also occurred before the U.S. Embassy in Moscow on the 24th, the demonstrators, school children, showed no signs of getting out of hand, and the affair had clearly not been engineered.

By this time Khrushchev seems to have decided on a course of action. While avoiding any showdown, he apparently sought to maintain tension and thus prepare both the American public and its government for a compromise. Early that evening in Moscow, the Soviet radio broadcast the Premier's reply to an appeal from Bertrand Russell. The Soviet Government, wrote Khrushchev, "will not take any reckless decisions, will not permit itself to be provoked by the unwarranted actions of the United States of America and will do everything to eliminate the situation fraught with irreparable consequences which has arisen in connection with the aggressive actions of the United States Government. We shall do everything in our power to prevent war from breaking out." At the same time the Soviet Premier appealed to Western public opinion to put pressure on Washington. What is needed now, he continued, "is not only the efforts of the Soviet Union, the Socialist countries and Cuba . . . but also the efforts of all states, all peoples and all segments of society to avert a military catastrophe." But the message contained one very tough passage: Should the United States carry out "the program of piratic actions outlined by it, we shall have to resort to means of defense against an aggressor to defend our rights . . . We have no other way out."[5]

Khrushchev emphasized the tough line in a conversation with an American businessman, Mr. William E. Knox, the same day. Mr. Knox, president of Westinghouse Electric International Company, in Moscow for business talks with Soviet officials, was summoned to the Kremlin at 2:00 P.M. on the 24th; he was ushered into Khrushchev's office at 3:30, and a three-hour conversation ensued.

The Soviet Premier decried the President's comparative youth. Despite his differences with the former President, he was sure General Eisenhower would have handled the Cuban situation in a much more mature manner. Whether because of the pending election or the President's youth, Mr. Kennedy had embarked on a very dangerous policy. Khrushchev, Mr. Knox later wrote, "seemed very conscious of the age gap . . . At one point, he remarked that one difficulty in the way of successful negotiation was the fact that his eldest son, for example, is older than the American President."

The Soviet Premier's tone on Cuba during this conversation was generally hard. Soviet freighters were unarmed, he said, and American ships might stop one or two. But if they did, he would order Soviet submarines to sink the blockading vessels. (Soviet submarines were quite numerous in the Caribbean during the crisis; the U.S. Navy detected and tracked at least six. But the Navy apparently considered the concentration nothing more than an excellent opportunity to test the latest sonar equipment and antisubmarine tactics in general.) The Soviet Union, declared Khrushchev, had indeed sent antiaircraft and surface-to-surface missiles to Cuba, together with both conventional and nuclear warheads. Soviet officers controlled all of these sophisticated weapons and would fire them only on his orders, but if Washington wanted to find out how well Cuba was defended, it need only initiate an attack. "He then said he was not interested in the destruction of the world, but if we all wanted to meet in hell, it was up to us."

In seeking this interview, Khrushchev evidently meant to cow the American public and administration with several blustering statements, statements which were not made in an official release or note and could easily be denied later if necessary. At the end of the talk he assured his visitor that he might tell the press everything about the conversation. But not until November 18 (in the *New York Times Magazine*) did Mr. Knox give a full account of the meeting. After reporting the details to the State Department, he spoke briefly

with reporters in Washington on October 26. "These are critical times," he said, "and I don't believe it would be helpful
to say more."

Reconnaissance photos on the 25th showed work on the
missile sites proceeding at an accelerated pace. And on the
morning of the 26th the Soviet press published a rather ominous reply to an appeal of the previous day by U Thant, Acting Secretary General of the United Nations. We have, wrote
Khrushchev, "ordered the masters of Soviet vessels bound for
Cuba but not yet within the area of the American warships'
piratical activities to stay out of the interception area, as you
recommend." But, continued the Premier, the other side
must understand "that such a situation, in which we keep
vessels immobilized on the high seas, must be a purely temporary one; the period cannot under any circumstances be of
long duration."[6]

In the message to Lord Russell, Khrushchev said he would
"consider useful a top-level meeting," and he also told Mr.
Knox he was anxious for a meeting with President Kennedy,
in Moscow, Washington, at sea, or in some neutral city. And
the next day Seymour Topping reported Soviet sources in
Moscow as saying their Premier hoped President Kennedy
would accept the invitation to a summit. Whether or not
Khrushchev really wanted a meeting, a positive reaction
might indicate some wavering in the President's determination—but Washington ignored the bid.

By October 26, the Soviet Premier was clearly worried and
was seeking a face-saving formula for a retreat. At 1:30 that
afternoon, Alexander S. Fomin, counselor of the Soviet Embassy in Washington, called John Scali, the diplomatic correspondent of the American Broadcasting Company, and asked

for an immediate meeting. Fomin, the Soviet intelligence chief in the United States, had his own lines of communication to Moscow. He had lunched with Mr. Scali several times previously and knew that he was trusted at the highest American governmental levels.

When the two men met at the Occidental Restaurant, Fomin asked Scali to sound out his high-level friends at the State Department on a possible solution of the crisis. The one he proposed was what both parties eventually accepted: withdrawal of the Soviet missiles, U.N. inspection in Cuba, and an American pledge not to invade the island. Fomin also suggested that Ambassador Adlai Stevenson might discuss the matter with the Soviet representative at the United Nations.

And that evening a long rambling message from Khrushchev to the President began to arrive at the State Department. It had apparently been composed at the same time as Fomin's instructions. The Soviet Premier admitted the presence of missiles in Cuba but declared that they would never be used in an attack on the United States. "We are of sound mind and understand perfectly well that if we attack you, you will respond the same way." He had sent the missiles to Cuba to protect that country, continued Khrushchev. Thus, "if assurances were given that the President of the United States would not participate in an attack on Cuba and the blockade lifted, then the question of the removal or the destruction of the missile sites in Cuba would then be an entirely different question."

After leaving Fomin, Mr. Scali had gone directly to Roger Hilsman at the State Department and typed up a summary of the conversation. After reading it and consulting the other

Presidential advisers, Secretary Rusk took the reporter to the White House where President Kennedy instructed him to give the Soviet official an affirmative reply. Rusk wrote out the text in his own handwriting: "I have reason to believe that the USG [U.S. Government] sees real possibilities and supposes that the representatives of the two governments in New York could work this matter out with U Thant and with each other. My impression is, however, that time is very urgent." Mr. Scali was also authorized to say that the statement came from the "highest levels in the government of the United States."

Scali met the Soviet official again at 7:35 P.M. in the coffee shop of the Statler Hilton Hotel. Satisfied that he was actually hearing the views of very high officials, Fomin immediately tried to haggle and suggested inspection of U.S. bases in Florida in view of the proposed inspections in Cuba. He could not speak for his government, replied Scali, but he felt the President would reject any such proposal; the network reporter also stressed the urgency and danger of the situation. The Soviet official then thanked Scali, emphasized that the information would be passed immediately to the highest levels in Moscow, and hurried away.[7]

This reply was Kennedy's only tactical mistake of the crisis, if mistake it was. At the time the situation was tense, but not yet tense enough to preclude bargaining. Fomin's offer and Khrushchev's hint in the message of the 26th represented the first moves in the bargaining process. By definition, the concessions the Soviet Premier offered were not the maximum concessions he was prepared to make. Instead they were the minimum concessions he thought the United States might accept. The President's eagerness and the "real possibilities" he saw in the offer apparently convinced Khrushchev that a few more threatening gestures would induce Washington to accept even less. Conceivably, however, Nikita Sergeyevich may simply have lost his nerve. Once satisfied that he had a face-saving out, he may have recovered enough of it to try for something better.

The next day, the 27th, the Moscow radio made several announcements of an important broadcast scheduled for 5:00 P.M. At that hour a message for President Kennedy was delivered to the U.S. Embassy and the radio began broadcasting its text. "You are worried over Cuba," wrote Khrushchev.

You say that it worries you because it lies at a distance of 90 miles across the sea from the shores of the United States. However, Turkey lies next to us. Our sentinels are pacing up and down and watching each other. . . . You have stationed devastating rocket weapons, which you call offensive, in Turkey literally right next to us. . . . This is why I make this proposal: We agree to remove those weapons from Cuba which you regard as offensive weapons. We agree to do this and to state this commitment in the United Nations. Your representatives will make a statement to the effect that the United States, on its part, bearing in mind the anxiety and concern of the Soviet state, will evacuate its analogous weapons from Turkey.[8]

This "offer" was broadcast at 10:00 A.M. Washington time. Shortly thereafter a Soviet rocket battery, manned by Soviet personnel, shot down an American U-2 plane over Cuba. The pilot, Major Rudolf Anderson, Jr., of the 4080th Strategic Reconnaissance Wing, United States Air Force, was killed. And other antiaircraft batteries fired on low-flying reconnaissance aircraft.[9]

The Soviet Premier wrote the script for his short melo-

drama—perhaps animated cartoon would be a better term—
for two main characters: a large, vicious, and hungry tomcat
(to be played by Nikita S. Khrushchev, Chairman of the
Council of Ministers and First Secretary of the Communist
Party of the U.S.S.R.) and a small, thoroughly frightened
mouse (to be played by John F. Kennedy, President of the
United States). Act one opens with the mouse cornered but
the cat hesitating to close in. After a few threatening gestures, the cat murmurs to himself, but loud enough for the
mouse to hear, "got to watch that mouse hole in the baseboard." He then moves aside slightly to expose the mouse
hole—the Turkish-Cuban base exchange offer—and immediately pounces (shooting down the U-2 and firing on the
other planes) but misses by a mouse whisker. At this point,
with a squeak of mingled terror and relief, the mouse is supposed to scuttle into the hole—and into a very secure trap
concealed behind the baseboard.

To the uninformed, the offer to exchange Cuban for Turkish bases seemed very reasonable. But any indication of
American willingness to take part in such a deal would have
been worse than tolerating the Soviet build-up in Cuba.
"Can the United States," asked Max Frankel in Washington
on the 27th, "enter into worldwide deals with the Soviet
Union without doing grave injury to its military alliances and
to its reputation as the defender of allied and not just national interests?" Of course not! Once convinced that Washington was not to be depended upon, America's allies would
have no choice but to seek the best terms possible from Moscow, even in the event of a direct Soviet threat to their national existence. Thus N.A.T.O. and the other elements of
the Western coalition would join France's East European al-

liances of the interwar years on the rubbish heap of history.

Nikita Sergeyevich had thought up a very clever scheme indeed. And if, as seems likely, he was playing the situation strictly "by ear," this fact makes his display of cunning still more remarkable. The plan had only one weakness—it didn't work! But it might easily have worked a year earlier when Washington had quailed at the prospect of a showdown at the Friedrichstrasse crossing in Berlin.

And even in October 1962, Khrushchev had good reason to expect a successful outcome. On October 23 Max Frankel had reported some ill-advised remarks by Washington officials: "Some sources said that if the Russians wished to engage in negotiations for the dismantling of offensive missile bases in Cuba, it was conceivable that the United States might be willing to dismantle one of the obsolescent American bases near Soviet territory." Polaris-equipped submarines had greatly reduced the need for such bases, and "a Thor missile base in Britain already was being dismantled. Questions have been raised here about the need for bases in Italy. . . . The most serious disagreement here centers on the continued necessity for bases in Turkey." And in his column of the 25th, Walter Lippmann had urged that the United States try "to negotiate a face-saving agreement . . . The only place that is truly comparable with Cuba is Turkey. This is the only place where there are strategic weapons right on the frontier of the Soviet Union." (In a third conversation with Scali on the 27th, Fomin mentioned this column and two days later, after the crisis was over, complained that it was "difficult to understand how Walter Lippmann, a close friend of the President, can be wrong.")[10]

Between 1,000 and 1,500 persons were picketing the

White House at midafternoon on the 27th. Some groups advocated compromise while others urged a strong stand. But the Student Peace Union, according to Cabell Phillips of the *New York Times*, "had by far the largest number of demonstrators and occupied the choice position on the sidewalk, immediately in front of the White House." The peace pickets carried hand-lettered placards reading, e.g., "Disarm Under World Law," "Peace, Si! Stick, No!" "We Must not Invade Cuba," and "End This Madness." Peace Union members also distributed a mimeographed leaflet in which they protested "a wholly misguided and reckless response to the [Soviet] threat on the part of our country. The only answer lies in an attitude of conciliation and honest bargaining." Admittedly, mush-minds of this variety can cause a stir and attract attention almost in inverse relation to their intelligence and judgment. Nevertheless, according to Mr. Phillips, both sides, the pacifists and those urging a hard line, "seemed agreed at midday that an exchange of United States bases in Turkey for Soviet bases in Cuba, as Premier Khrushchev had proposed, probably was as good a solution as any they could think of."

But President Kennedy, who had learned a few things since January 1961, didn't share this view. During the afternoon of the 27th, the White House released a statement on the latest Soviet proposal: No negotiations could proceed under the immediate threat posed by the missiles, and "as an urgent preliminary to consideration of any proposals, work on the Cuban bases must stop; offensive weapons must be rendered inoperable and further shipment of offensive weapons to Cuba must cease—all under effective international verification.

"As to the proposals concerning the security of nations outside this hemisphere, the United States and its allies have long taken the lead in seeking properly inspected arms limitation on both sides. These efforts can continue as soon as the present Soviet-created threat is ended."[11]

In other words, Nikita Sergeyevich, no swap!

Acting on Secretary Rusk's instructions, Scali met Fomin once again at 4:15 that afternoon. The Soviet official was puzzled and unhappy and attempted to explain the difference in the Soviet offers of the 26th and 27th as the result of communication difficulties, i.e. delayed reception in Moscow of his report on the favorable American reaction on the 26th. At this the network correspondent exploded, calling the Soviet maneuvers a "stinking double-cross." After warning Fomin that time was critically short and the Turkish-Cuban exchange completely unacceptable, Scali reported back to the State Department.

Having read and considered the dictated report on this conversation, the President and his advisers decided to interpret, ostensibly, Khrushchev's message of the 26th as agreement to a compromise. A message to this effect was drafted, dispatched, and released to the press and radio early in the evening of the 27th: "As I read your letter," wrote Mr. Kennedy, "the key elements of your proposal—which seem generally acceptable as I understand them—are as follows:

"1) You would agree to remove these weapons systems from Cuba under appropriate United Nations observation and supervision; and undertake, with suitable safeguards, to halt the further introduction of such weapons systems into Cuba.

"2) We, on our part, would agree—upon the establishment

of adequate arrangements through the United Nations, to insure the carrying out and continuation of these commitments —(a) to remove promptly the quarantine measures now in effect and (b) to give assurances against an invasion of Cuba."

The most important factor, the President warned, was "cessation of work on missile sites in Cuba and measures to render such weapons inoperable, under effective international guarantees." Any continuation of this threat or any attempt to link the problem to the question of European or world security "would surely lead to an intensification of the Cuban crisis and a grave risk to the peace of the world."

As the message was being dispatched, Robert F. Kennedy was stressing the seriousness of the situation to Soviet Ambassador Dobrynin whom he had invited to his Justice Department office. Reconnaissance flights over Cuba would continue, the Attorney General warned, and if planes were fired on the fire would be returned. "We had to have a commitment by tomorrow that those [missile] bases would be removed. I was not giving them an ultimatum but a statement of fact. He should understand that if they did not remove those bases, we would remove them." The Attorney General then informed the ambassador of the President's latest message to Khrushchev and said there could be no agreement under threat or pressure on removing missiles from Turkey.[12]

As we have seen, on the 26th the Soviet Premier was probably prepared to go beyond Fomin's offer. And by the evening of the 27th the situation was more tense and threatening, as seen from Moscow, than it had been the day before. Indeed, military evidence of American determination had been accumulating for several days: "All inquiries brought the same essential response:" reported Max Frankel from Washington as early as the 25th, "that the objective was the dismantling of Soviet bases in the Western hemisphere and that further measures would be taken if no satisfaction could be obtained." And another *New York Times* reporter, Jack Raymond, wrote in a similar vein the same day: "The Pentagon refused comment on reports that the mounting military build-up in Florida was in preparation for an invasion or bombardment of ballistic missile sites in Cuba."

The next day the White House announced evidence of continued work on the intermediate-range missile sites, "at a rapid pace," and "progressive refinements" of the medium-range positions. "High officials," wrote E. W. Kenworthy that evening in Washington, "said that such work could not be allowed to continue indefinitely." Mr. Kenworthy reported "the impression in the capital that the Government was looking . . . toward the possibility of further direct action by the United States." The most likely move was a total blockade which would cut off oil, food, machinery, and spare parts. But Washington was also considering bombing of the missile sites. And a Pentagon spokesman again refused to comment "on reports that a massive military force was building up in Florida for the possible bombardment of missile sites in Cuba or an invasion of the island" (Jack Raymond).

At the United Nations on the 27th, Adlai E. Stevenson spoke with the delegates of thirteen N.A.T.O. and other friendly countries. According to the accounts Thomas J. Hamilton of the *New York Times* received from "reliable sources," "military action contemplated, if no way was found to stop the development of the bases, would be in the form of an air strike," and "other dependable sources" said Mr.

Stevenson had conferred at length with Latin-American delegates to obtain approval of the Organization of American States for such an air strike. On the night of the 26th, "some Latin-American delegates were given the impression that an air attack . . . was due in a matter of hours." Although the atmosphere had improved somewhat, "they still thought that such action was likely quite soon." ("We received information from Cuban comrades and from other sources on the morning of October 27," Khrushchev told the Supreme Soviet on December 12, "directly stating that this attack [on Cuba] would be carried out in the next two or three days.")

At about noon Washington time, also on the 27th, the pilot of an Alaska-based U-2 returning from a routine air-sampling mission over the Pole made a navigational error and flew over the Chukchi Peninsula, that part of Siberia lying across the Bering Strait from Alaska. Soviet fighters took off to intercept the plane, and the American pilot radioed for help —in the clear. Fighters in Alaska then took off to meet the U-2 and escort it home. "What is this—a provocation?" asked the Soviet Premier in a message of the 28th. Such an overflight, he complained, "can be easily taken for a nuclear bomber and this might push us to a fateful step." Nikita Sergeyevich was exaggerating, of course, but the incident may very well have given him a few bad moments.

At 3:30 that afternoon, following reports from Havana that reconnaissance aircraft had been fired on, Arthur Sylvester, Assistant Secretary of Defense for Public Affairs, read a prepared statement to reporters: "Any interference with such surveillance [of Cuba] will meet counter-action and surveillance will be enforced." For several days reconnaissance fighters of the 363rd Tactical Reconnaissance Wing

145

had been making tree-top level sorties at very high speeds. The commanders of the Soviet antiaircraft batteries, unable to fire effectively on planes flying at such high speeds and low altitude, must have realized and reported their own vulnerability to bombing by napalm, high explosive, or even tactical atom bombs. Shortly after 10:00 P.M. Secretary of Defense McNamara issued a statement warning it was "essential that such reconnaissance flights continue." The continued build-up in Cuba and the possibility of further attacks on American aircraft "require that we be prepared for any eventuality." The Air Force had therefore been instructed to call twenty-four troop carrier squadrons to active duty.[13]

At this point the Soviet Premier had three choices: He could (1) start an all-out nuclear war; (2) await intensification of the blockade or, more likely, bombing of the missile bases followed eventually by an American invasion of Cuba. In this case, instead of TASS distributing photos of rockets aimed at Washington, the Associated Press, United Press International, and other Western news agencies might soon be passing out pictures of Soviet gunners being marched away to American prisoner-of-war camps. (3) The third choice was to back down while he still didn't have too far to go. Thus at 9:00 A.M. Washington time, on October 28, 1962, the Soviet radio broadcast a message from Khrushchev to President Kennedy: "The Soviet Government, in addition to earlier instructions on the discontinuation of further work on weapons construction sites, has given a new order to dismantle the weapons, which you describe as offensive, and to crate and return them to the Soviet Union." And further, "we are prepared to reach agreement to enable representatives of the United Nations to verify the dismantling of these means."

The President replied in a message released to the press and radio that afternoon, before all of the text of Khrushchev's communication had arrived through official channels: "I hope that the necessary measures can at once be taken through the United Nations, as your message says, so that the United States in turn will be able to remove the quarantine measures now in effect."[14]

That morning, an hour or so after Khrushchev's message, the Cuban radio had broadcast Castro's terms for a settlement of the crisis (since known as Fidel's Five Points): (1) ending of the American economic blockade and other restrictions, (2) ending of subversive activities against the Castro regime, (3) ending of "pirate attacks" from bases in the United States and Puerto Rico, (4) "The end of all violations of air and naval space," and (5) "Withdrawal from the naval base at Guantanamo and the return of this Cuban territory occupied by the United States."[15] From Moscow the next day, Seymour Topping reported "some hesitation" in publishing Castro's demands. "The Moscow radio did not broadcast the text last night, as it did the text of President Kennedy's message welcoming the understanding with Premier Khrushchev." *Izvestia* published the Cuban statment on the 29th, but under the headline, "Suggestions of Fidel Castro."

The same evening in Washington, the White House announced the temporary suspension of the blockade at the request of U Thant. The Acting Secretary General of the United Nations was to fly to Havana on the 30th for two days of talks, and he reportedly felt such a suspension might facilitate discussion of United Nations' inspection measures. The next day, for the same reason, Washington announced a two-day suspension of reconnaissance flights over Cuba. But the day before, the 29th, light antiaircraft batteries, probably

Cuban, had fired on an RF-101. Some people in Moscow may have misinterpreted the developments of the 29th and 30th. Referring to Fidel's Five Points, *Izvestia* on the 31st declared, "The fulfillment of these demands is essential for the security of Cuba." As Seymour Topping pointed out, "the initial cautious treatment by Soviet news media of the Castro demands as merely 'suggestions' now has taken the form of outright support." But that night the White House announced resumption the next day of air surveillance and the blockade. It also announced cancellation of a Presidential news conference scheduled for the following afternoon. Although reporters interpreted this action as a sign of renewed tension, the two announcements apparently convinced Moscow of Fidel's limitations as a pointer. Soviet spokesmen continued to support the Cuban demands, but the support was obviously *pro forma.*

Reconnaissance planes took new photographs on November 1, and the President spoke over television the following evening: The photos and other indications, he said, revealed "that the Soviet missile bases in Cuba are being dismantled, their missiles and related equipment are being crated and the fixed installations at these sites are being destroyed." But the United States, Mr. Kennedy continued, "intends to follow closely the completion of this work through a variety of means, including aerial surveillance, until such time as an equally satisfactory international means of verification is effected."

Castro, however, was still in a position to veto any "equally satisfactory international means of verification." U Thant had taken eighteen United Nations officials to Havana with him, and five others flew from New York on the morning of October 31. The U.N. leader had planned to leave some of his aides in Cuba as the nucleus of an inspection corps. But the whole party returned to New York on the evening of the 31st. The same day Moscow disclosed that Anastas I. Mikoyan, Khrushchev's right-hand man, would fly to Cuba the next day on an urgent mission. And on November 1 Castro himself revealed the details of the talks with U Thant in which he had declared he would permit no inspectors on Cuban territory. "Sources here," reported Max Frankel from Washington on November 3, "said no satisfactory ideas or proposals had yet been made by the Soviet or Cuban Governments about international inspection . . . Until such investigation is effective, they said, United States planes will continue to fly daily on extensive reconnaissance missions over Cuban territory."

Castro remained adamant, and on the 7th U.S. and Soviet representatives at the United Nations agreed that the U.S. Navy would check Soviet ships leaving Cuba to verify the number of missiles removed. The next day the Department of Defense announced photographic evidence of the dismantling of "all known" offensive-missile bases; many of the missiles had already been loaded aboard ship, and some of the ships had sailed. The Navy began checking the departing ships at sea the same day, and, speaking on a television program on the 11th, Deputy Defense Secretary Roswell L. Gilpatric disclosed that the Navy had counted forty-two medium-range missiles. Nevertheless, Moscow had not fully carried out its pledges. Thirty or more IL-28 bombers remained in Cuba and must also be removed.

But Khrushchev and Castro were to fight at least one rear-guard diplomatic action. On November 15, U Thant handed over to U.S. representatives a Soviet-Cuban memorandum for settling the outstanding issues. The memo seems to have been merely a rehash of Fidel's Five Points: lifting of the blockade, a pledge by the United States not to invade Cuba, withdrawal of the U.S. forces concentrated in the South Atlantic states, no aggression or subversion against Cuba from the United States or Latin America, and no interference with Cuban trade. In a letter delivered to the Acting Secretary General the same day, the Cuban Premier warned that "to the extent of the fire power of our anti-aircraft weapons, any warplane which violates the sovereignty of Cuba, by invading our air space, can only do so at the risk of being destroyed." In New York that evening, U.S. representatives warned Soviet officials that serious consequences could follow any interference with the reconnaissance flights, and the next day Washington officials promised "appropriate measures" to protect the aircraft.

And from Washington on the 19th, Tad Szulc of the *New York Times* reported additional evidence of the administration's determination: "President Kennedy is considering warning the Soviet Union and Cuba tomorrow that the United States will be forced to take stringent measures if Soviet jet bombers are not removed from Cuba promptly. Administration officials indicated tonight that Mr. Kennedy might use his news conference at 6 P.M. tomorrow to announce what additional steps the United States was contemplating." At 1:00 the next morning, a letter from Castro was delivered to U Thant. The jet bombers, said the Cuban Premier, were too old [and to sour?] to be useful to Cuba. "If the Soviet Government considers that the withdrawal of such planes would benefit the negotiations and contribute to a solution of the crisis, the revolutionary Government of Cuba will not be an obstacle to that decision."

In Washington the same evening, of November 20, President Kennedy began his news conference with a prepared statement: 'I have today been informed by Chairman Khrushchev that all of the IL-28 bombers now in Cuba will be withdrawn in 30 days. He also agreed that these planes can be observed and counted as they leave. Inasmuch as this goes a long way towards reducing the danger which faced this hemisphere four weeks ago, I have this afternoon instructed the Secretary of Defense to lift our naval quarantine." But as the President pointed out, the Cuban Government had not yet agreed to United Nations inspection and the United States had no guarantee against subsequent introduction of missiles and bombers. "Consequently, if the Western Hemisphere is to continue to be protected against offensive weapons, this Government has no choice but to pursue its own means of checking on military activities in Cuba." Aerial reconnaissance, in other words, would continue.

Shipment of the bombers began as early as December 1; four days later Soviet representatives at the United Nations furnished Adlai Stevenson a schedule listing ships, sailing dates, and the number of aircraft involved. Finally, on December 6, the Department of Defense announced the withdrawal of the last of the bombers.

But what had been happening in Germany in the meantime? Of one thing we may be sure: The President and his advisers were very seriously concerned about possible Soviet action against West Berlin. In his address of October 22, Mr. Kennedy had warned that "this latest Soviet threat or any other threat which is made either independently or in response to our actions this week must and will be met with determination. Any hostile move anywhere in the world against the safety and freedom of peoples to whom we are committed including in particular the brave people of West Berlin will be met by whatever action is needed."

At about 11:00 P.M. (local time) on October 22, East-zone guards began delaying trucks leaving Berlin for West Germany. But apparently this represented merely routine unpleasantness, and after about three hours traffic was allowed to move without interruption. Three days later a British battalion traveled from West Germany to Berlin without incident. Officials in West Berlin said Soviet authorities had cleared the British convoys "with unusual speed"; on the 27th Allied officers declared that the Russians had cleared military convoys "swiftly and correctly" since the beginning of the Cuban crisis and they were having "less trouble than ever." The day before, however, the 26th, East German guards had delayed civilian trucks en route to West Berlin, as long as four hours in some cases, but traffic returned to normal on the 27th. Trucks were again delayed during the night of October 31 and the following morning but traveled without hindrance later in the day. On November 1 and 2, Soviet officers delayed small U.S. Army convoys, for half an hour on the 1st and eighty minutes on the 2nd, on the grounds they had not received advance notification. On the 3rd, however, a small convoy went through without any difficulty even though no notification had been given. Two more small American convoys traveled the autobahn without incident on the 15th, again without advance notice.

Sydney Gruson summed up the absence of post-Cuba developments in a dispatch from Bonn on November 17: "Contrary to everyone's expectations, the Cuban crisis produced a lull in the Berlin crisis . . . the pressure against West Berlin eased. There was a sudden halt in the Communist propaganda about the imminence of a separate peace treaty that might force a showdown with the Allies. There was no buzzing of Allied planes in the air corridors. With rare exceptions, both Allied and West German civilian traffic moved smoothly."

By the end of November, Soviet troops were reported patrolling the borders of West Berlin, and East German border guards seemed somewhat reluctant to fire on fugitives. According to a press dispatch of December 4, West Berlin officials "said the number of successful escapes had increased in the last few weeks. Reliable estimates say 10 to 20 persons managed to cross every night."[16] Soviet authorities had reportedly overruled the East-zone regime's shoot-to-kill policy, but even without a change in orders East German guards may have hesitated to open fire. "After all," they must have thought, "yesterday Khrushchev backed down over Cuba. Tomorrow he may back down over East Germany. Then where will we be?"

After a two-day stay, Foreign Minister Gromyko left East Berlin for home on October 24 without having made any threatening statements regarding a peace treaty. And Khrushchev himself made a very cautious remark on the subject, at a Kremlin reception on November 7, when a reporter asked about a possible deadline for a German treaty. "I have been reading a lot about schedules and so on," he replied. "But that is not the question. It is just like the time of birth. When the time is ripe the child is born."[17]

In reporting on the November 7 celebrations of the anniversary of the Revolution, Seymour Topping remarked on the mild tone regarding Berlin: In the speeches by the Soviet Premier and those of Defense Minister Malinovsky at the Red Square parade, and also by First Deputy Premier A. N. Kosygin at a Party meeting the day before, "there have been no renewals of the Soviet threats about Berlin . . . The familiar warning that a separate peace treaty abrogating the Western rights in Berlin would be signed with East Germany unless the West comes to terms had not been repeated. There has been no mention either of the demand that allied troops leave West Berlin."

On the 29th the Soviet Government protested court action in West Berlin against a Communist-front organization, but the note was comparatively mild: "Everything taking place in West Berlin graphically confirms the degree to which the necessity of a German peace settlement and normalization of the situation in West Berlin have become urgent."

The East German Communist Party issued a long-range Party program on the weekend of November 25—a program which contained no mention of a separate peace treaty. And in a speech on December 2, Ulbricht emphasized the need for compromise: "It is necessary to realize that peaceful coexistence means making compromises on both sides," he declared. "We have adopted a long-term policy," he continued, "a policy of peaceful coexistence in Germany that is to lead to a German peace treaty, a confederation [of East and West Germany] and eventually—along this sole remaining path—toward reunification."[18]

Finally, addressing a Party congress in East Berlin on January 16, 1963, Khrushchev displayed an attitude very similar to the sour-grapes attitude Soviet spokesmen had adopted af-

ter the March stand-down. Although four years had passed
since the question of a German peace treaty was first raised,
"much water has flowed under the bridge and substantial
changes have taken place." The sector boundary in Berlin
had been "like an open gate, which subversive forces used
unhindered and with impunity . . . to undermine the very
foundations of socialism." The sealing off of East Berlin represented "a most important step in strengthening the sovereignty of the German Democratic Republic. It became in
fact the real master and guard of its frontiers and obtained
the possibility of reliably protecting its citizens' socialist
gains and peaceful labor from external encroachments."

The Soviet Premier then went on to quote an apocryphal
conversation between a Russian and an American journalist.
"True, a peace treaty has not been signed," said Nikita Sergeyevich's American, "but you have almost completely attained the goal that you pursued in insisting on its conclusion. You have closed the border, you have cut off the access
of the West to the German Democratic Republic. Thus even
before signing a peace treaty you have obtained what you
sought and what you wanted to get through concluding this
treaty." And in addition "you have also gained the opportunity to step on the corns of the West. The lanes of access to
West Berlin through the territory of the German Democratic
Republic are such corns."

"Not everything here is exact," Khrushchev remarked,
"but the American journalist comes close to the truth." Although the Soviet Premier felt impelled to conclude with
some rather threatening remarks about the treaty, they were
quite vague and evidently intended merely as notice that the
Soviet claim had not been completely abandoned.[19]

When President Kennedy briefed Congressional leaders two hours before his speech of October 22, Senator Richard Russell, Chairman of the Armed Services Committee, declared that the President had adopted a course which would take longest, annoy the most countries, and achieve the least. At the time, this writer would have agreed with the senator— and would have added that it was the course most likely to invite Soviet reprisals against Berlin. A quick and successful invasion, on the other hand, would present Khrushchev with a *fait accompli* rather than tempt him to apply a Berlin blockade to force abandonment of the Cuban one. But in meeting the threat to Berlin head on, Mr. Kennedy disarmed it. In adopting exactly the course of action the Berlin "crisis" was ideally designed to preclude, he proved it useless as a threat. The subsequent mild Soviet tone on Berlin and a separate peace treaty undoubtedly reflected some instinctive caution. Kremlin authorities have a great deal of experience in staging parades and demonstrations, however, and realize that once a parade is over the banners, bunting, placards, etc. should be hauled away promptly.

The concluding paragraph of Chapter 5, the reference to the proverb about grasping nettles, was written in June 1962. Although President Kennedy grasped the Berlin nettle more firmly than the writer would have recommended on October 22, he certainly demonstrated the applicability of the proverb.

8

1963, Year of the Indisposed Devil

As EMPHASIZED earlier, every Soviet citizen born before 1930 or 1935 has bitter memories of the suffering endured during World War II, and the desire for peace has been universal and profound. Thus, the second best political gambit in the Soviet Union in the decade following Stalin's death was to play upon this general fear of another war. (The most effective, as Nikita Sergeyevich demonstrated, was to kick Stalin's bones.) Although the regime managed to avoid a general war-scare at the time of the Cuban crisis, the upper ranks of Soviet society, factory managers, army officers, Party and government officials, must have soon realized the dangerous situation brought about by Khrushchev's miscalculation.

And the Cuban fiasco seems to have encouraged the Premier's opponents, led by Frol R. Kozlov, in the Party Presidium. Even Khrushchev's followers in that body couldn't be trusted fully. As pointed out before, Soviet leaders can count on personal loyalties only when their own positions appear secure. Dimitri T. Shepilov, for example, the former foreign minister who was generally considered Khrushchev's protégé, joined the "anti-Party" group in 1957. Perhaps the only reliable ways of ensuring loyalty are terror or general popular acceptance. And terror may be too dangerous to even attempt. In 1936 Stalin's followers complacently observed with approval the trials of the anti-Stalin opposition leaders; in 1937–38 they were the most surprised of all to find themselves in the cellars of the N.K.G.B. As every Soviet citizen in a responsible position now realizes, and as Khrushchev himself disclosed, once a purge starts no one is safe. Significantly, a few months after his death the one person against whom Stalin's other heirs united, almost instinctively, was Beria who controlled the police. And during the first half of 1963, in a campaign for conformity in literature and the arts, the Party was clearly reluctant to go beyond exhortations and warnings.[1]

In any event, Khrushchev evidently considered popular acceptance the only feasible personal insurance, and at the end of 1962 embarked on a campaign to refurbish, both at home and abroad, the image of Nikita Sergeyevich, the Sensible Old Peacemonger. (At the same time, since the adulation rendered up to Stalin before 1953 was still too well remembered, he also sought to avoid any appearance of a "personality cult" of his own. The November 16, 1962 issue of the *Vedomosti* [Bulletin] of the Supreme Soviet revealed that the town of "Khrushchev" in the Ukraine had been renamed "Kremges." And on several occasions during the first months of 1963, the regime and the Soviet Premier himself went out of their way to emphasize the "collective" nature of the leadership.[2])

Since 1962 the Chinese have repeatedly claimed that the

Sino-Soviet conflict really started at the Twentieth Soviet Party-Congress, in February 1956, with Khrushchev's "secret" anti-Stalin speech. And this claim can hardly be refuted: Once Nikita Sergeyevich realized the political capital implicit in anti-Stalinism, it was only a question of time until he began attacking the foreign Communist Party still practicing Stalinism in all its severity.

In 1958 Peking embarked on its "Great Leap Forward" (i.e. merciless forced-industrialization at the expense of an already marginal living standard) and began establishing "people's communes," vast forced-labor organizations enrolling most of the rural population. As the Chinese Communists later complained, and as it was known in the West at the time, Soviet leaders soon began to disparage the program. "These attacks were almost invariably led by Khrushchev himself. He insinuated that China's Socialist construction was 'skipping over a stage' and was 'equalitarian Communism' and that China's people's communes were 'in essence reactionary.'" (*Jenmin Jih Pao* article of September 6, 1963.) In a reply of September 21, *Izvestia* admitted the truth of the charge, stating that the attacks had been made "precisely because the interests of the Chinese people are dear to us." The Soviet Communist Party, continued *Izvestia,* saw that the Great Leap and the communes represented "a road of dangerous experiments, a road of disregard for economic laws, for the experience of other Socialist states." On February 4, 1964 *Jenmin Jih Pao* went further, accusing Khrushchev of praising "Chinese anti-party elements for attacking the Chinese party's general line for Socialist construction, the big leap forward and the people's communes, describing their action as a 'manly act.'"

As the only consumer-goods item in plentiful supply during Stalin's rule, the knout formed a staple of the national diet. Adult Russians knew exactly what China's communes and "Great Leap Forward" meant in practice. For Nikita Sergeyevich to have endorsed or even kept silent about these developments would have been the equivalent of an American politician praising sin and condemning motherhood.

In July 1960 Moscow suddenly withdrew 1,390 Soviet technicians serving in China, abrogated 343 Sino-Soviet contracts, and canceled 257 joint scientific and technical projects (Chinese figures). Although the two parties soon began to make veiled press attacks on one another, signs of an open split began to appear only at the Twenty-Second Party Congress in Moscow in October 1961. Khrushchev's attack on Albania at this time was a not very indirect slap at Communist China, and was probably so interpreted by most Russians present and certainly by Chou En-lai who walked out.

A few days later, however, the United States Government backed down at the Friedrichstrasse in Berlin. Greatly encouraged by this sign of weakness, the Soviet Premier apparently decided that a *successful* campaign against Berlin would far outweigh any misgivings among the faint hearted at home; further attacks on the Chinese "warmongers" were therefore unnecessary for the time being. And this remained true once he had decided on the Cuban venture in July 1962. As late as October 14, only eight days before the Cuban crisis erupted, Khrushchev and most of the Party Presidium attended a farewell dinner for the departing Chinese Ambassador. At the time TASS reported a "friendly, warm and cordial atmosphere." According to a July 15, 1963 Open Letter of the Soviet Communist Party (and the truth of the statement was

admitted by the *Jenmin Jih Pao* article of September 6),
Khrushchev asked the ambassador to convey a formal Soviet
proposal to Mao Tse-tung: "To put aside all disputes and differences, not to try and establish who is right and who is
wrong, not to rake up the past, but to start our relations with
a clear page."

But the situation changed completely with the failure in
Cuba. "Since November, 1962," charged *Jenmin Jih Pao*
(September 6), "the leadership of the C.P.S.U. [Communist
Party of the Soviet Union] has launched still fiercer attacks—
on an international scale—against the Chinese Communist
Party . . . Khrushchev made one statement after another and
the Soviet press carried hundreds of articles attacking the
Chinese Communist Party on a whole set of issues." The
most important statements and articles during the last
months of 1962 and the first half of 1963 were, according to
the Chinese, Khrushchev's report to the Supreme Soviet on
December 12, 1962, a *Pravda* editorial of January 7, 1963, the
Soviet Premier's speech in Berlin on January 16, a *Pravda* editorial on February 10, and two letters from the Central
Committee of the Soviet Party dated February 21 and March
30.

In his speech to the Supreme Soviet, Khrushchev referred
to Albanian criticism of Moscow's conduct during the Cuban
crisis and complained that the Albanian leaders were attempting to egg the Soviet Government into provoking a
world war. Imperialism, he said, might be a "paper tiger" as
some quarters claimed, but it had atomic teeth and must be
treated cautiously. At the same time, he emphasized that the
Albanians were merely acting as the mouthpieces of other
"dogmatists" who had lost, or never had, faith in the peaceful

victory of communism and believed it could be achieved only through sacrificing millions of lives.

Communist China, the Soviet Premier pointed out, still tolerated "imperialist" colonies, Macao and Hong Kong, on its own doorstep, but the Soviet leaders had no intention of criticizing Peking for this. Alleging it was the result of increasing British and American support for India, he also recalled how the Chinese had broken off the trans-Himalayan campaign. But, said Khrushchev, some people might say that since the Chinese were withdrawing to their former positions they shouldn't have mounted the attack in the first place.[3]

The January 7 editorial in *Pravda* attacked the Albanians at length as the "most outspoken exponents" of "dogmatic and divisive views." And in Berlin nine days later Khrushchev again condemned the Albanian leaders who were "chattering about a nuclear-missile war," and also spoke of theoreticians who believed socialism could triumph only by a "war between states, through destruction, bloodshed and the deaths of millions of people." In conclusion, however, he appealed for a halt to polemics between the various Communist parties and an end to criticism of other parties within each party. Although not opposing in principle a general conference of Communist parties, the Soviet Premier urged that it be delayed for "passions to cool."

While attacking the Albanians for their intransigence, the February 10 *Pravda* editorial proclaimed the factors uniting the parties far greater and more important than those dividing them. Although a general conference was not advisable at the moment, the Soviet Communist Party was prepared for bilateral talks with any other party desiring them. And in its February 21 letter to Peking, the Soviet Central Committee warned of a bad effect the dispute was having on fraternal parties in capitalist countries; "enemies of socialism" were also attempting to exploit the differences in order to divide the Communist countries and split the "national liberation movement." Apparently Moscow feared a repetition of 1918–20 when under similar conditions the Bolsheviks had themselves disorganized and split the Social Democratic parties of the Second International. The Soviet Central Committee therefore urged a bilateral meeting of high-level representatives of both parties to discuss and reduce differences as much as possible; these talks would also create a favorable atmosphere for a future general conference.

The Chinese replied on March 9 (both letters were printed in *Pravda* and *Izvestia* on March 14 and 15 respectively). While condemning "Yugoslav revisionists," and stating that the Soviet Union must take the initiative in settling its dispute with Albania, the Chinese "welcomed" the proposal and invited Khrushchev to visit Peking. Should this be inconvenient, a delegation could be sent or a Chinese delegation could come to Moscow. In the meantime the Chinese Communist Party intended to suspend open replies in its press to previous Soviet attacks.

The Soviet Ambassador handed over the reply in Peking on April 2 (published in *Pravda* the next day): Khrushchev could not make the trip, but Mao would certainly be welcome in Moscow; if this was not feasible, the Soviet Central Committee suggested a meeting of delegations in Moscow around May 15. Although condemning the attitude of the Albanian leaders and defending the Yugoslavs, the Soviet Party again warned of the dangers of continued wrangling. The Soviet and Chinese Communist Parties were large and powerful and would suffer comparatively little, but the dispute would cause "great" and "unnecessary difficulties" for parties existing under "complicated conditions." While the Soviet press was also exercising restraint, the letter concluded, it could obviously find "more than a little to say" in reply to the latest "groundless attacks" in the Chinese press. Some additional exchanges between May 9 and 14 finally ended in agreement that a Chinese delegation would come to Moscow to start the talks on July 5, 1963. But in the meantime the climate of Moscow's relations with the West had been improving.

Desultory negotiations for a treaty banning atomic tests had started several years before President Kennedy assumed office, and at the beginning of 1963 were deadlocked over the question of inspections on Soviet territory. In Moscow on April 24 the British and U.S. ambassadors delivered appeals from the President and Prime Minister Macmillan for a new effort to reach an agreement. But at his press conference in Washington on May 8, Kennedy admitted having little hope and expressed fear of a new round of tests "if we don't get an agreement this year." "If we don't get it now," he continued, "I would think perhaps the genie is out of the bottle and we'll never get it back in again." The same day it was announced that three small underground tests in Nevada had been scheduled for later in the month.

Khrushchev's reply, delivered a few days later, gave the President little reason to change his opinion. And on May 13, in an English-language broadcast, the Moscow radio accused the United States of "imposing on the world a new round in the atomic arms race," of "starting a new round of tests in the atmosphere," and warned that the Soviet Union would not "stand by idly watching the U.S.A. perfect its nuclear weapons." Later in the day the Defense Department and the Atomic Energy Commission announced cancellation of the tests.

The Soviet Government, as President Kennedy admitted at a May 22 news conference, had not changed its position since the end of 1962. Yet it had seemed to him from the beginning that "unless we could get an agreement now, I would think the chance of getting it would be comparatively slight. We are, therefore, going to continue to push very hard in May and June and July, in every forum, to see if we can get an agreement." And on the 31st the British and U.S. embassies in Moscow delivered fresh appeals from the President and Prime Minister. A week later the Soviet Premier agreed to high-level talks in Moscow. Announcing the pending talks in a conciliatory speech at American University in Washington on June 10, President Kennedy stated that the United States would conduct no atmospheric tests as long as other states also refrained. And in an East Berlin speech of July 2, Khrushchev declared that while his government favored a ban on all tests, "this is now obviously impossible in view of the position of the Western powers"—i.e. their position on inspections to monitor underground testing. The Soviet Government was therefore willling to sign an agreement banning nuclear tests "in the atmosphere, in outer space and under water."[4]

But he also urged the "simultaneous signing of a nonaggression pact" between the N.A.T.O. and Warsaw Pact powers. With this second proposal, the Soviet Premier may have been attempting to sow dissension within N.A.T.O. As Max Frankel pointed out (July 4), the Germans "have supported

Washington's quest for a test-ban agreement, but they have remained suspicious of Washington's lingering interest in the nonaggression pledge."

Nikita Sergeyevich, in a jovial mood, personally opened the talks in Moscow on July 15—with newsmen present of course. Foreign Minister Gromyko headed the Soviet delegation while W. Averell Harriman and Lord Hailsham represented the United States and Britain. Although it was soon agreed to bypass the question of underground tests, apparently not until July 24 did Gromyko abandon his efforts for the simultaneous signing of the N.A.T.O.-Warsaw Pact nonaggression pledge. The test-ban protocol was initialed the following evening and a communiqué released at the same time mentioned the proposed nonaggression agreement: "The three governments have agreed fully to inform their respective allies in the two organizations concerning these talks and to consult with them about continuing discussions on this question with the purpose of achieving agreement satisfactory to all participants." And at a news conference held on the 27th, after his return to the United States, Mr. Harriman evidently considered it desirable to emphasize that "no commitments of any kind were taken, implied or otherwise, in regard to any matters that affected any of our allies."[5]

The treaty itself merely banned nuclear explosions in the air, in space, under water, or causing "radioactive debris to be present outside the territorial limits of the state under whose jurisdiction or control such explosion is conducted." And should "extraordinary events" jeopardize the "supreme interests" of one of the signatories, it could withdraw from the agreement after three months' notice. A large part of the protocol was devoted to the procedure for accession of other states, and a number of other governments did indeed accede. In this respect (as in others!) the test-ban treaty recalls the Kellogg antiwar pact of the 1920's.

Heading a large delegation which included six senators and Ambassador Adlai Stevenson, Secretary of State Rusk arrived in Moscow on August 3 for the formal signing of the treaty. As he pointed out in a statement upon arrival, "this is the first visit of an American Secretary of State to Moscow in sixteen years." The signing ceremony took place on August 5: "From the start of courtesy calls by the ministers [Lord Home, the British Foreign Secretary, was also on hand] at 9 A.M. to the end of the gala reception just before nightfall," reported Henry Tanner of the *New York Times*, the day "was filled with firm East-West handshakes, warm smiles, friendly jokes and toasts to 'peace and friendship' drunk in Soviet champagne." Reporters, photographers, and television cameras were of course present, and no one "smiled more broadly and clinked glasses more eagerly or more often than Premier Khrushchev. . . . Although he did not speak, he obviously assumed the role of host and, by implication, of chief architect of the treaty." The U.S. Senate ratified the agreement on September 24 and the Presidium of the Supreme Soviet on the following day.

While not intending to disrupt the world Communist movement, insofar as a "world movement" still existed, and for obvious domestic political advantages, Khrushchev may have intended to use the Chinese Communists merely temporarily as a whipping boy. The situation remained comparatively quiet during April and May, but on June 14 the Central Committee of the Chinese Communist Party addressed a lengthy letter to the Central Committee of the Soviet Party, a few days before a plenary session of the latter body. From an orthodox Communist point of view, the letter presented a sound, well-reasoned condemnation of Khrushchev's policies, and the language was fairly restrained, by later standards at least. One of the bitterest passages referred to the earlier Soviet accusation of "groundless attacks." "It is turning things upside down to describe articles replying to our attackers as 'attacks.'" Similarly, "If it is agreed that differences between fraternal parties should be settled through interparty consultations, then other fraternal parties should not be attacked publicly and by name at one's own congress or at other party congresses, in speeches by party leaders, resolutions, statements, etc; and still less should the ideological differences among fraternal parties be extended into the sphere of state relations."[6]

This letter certainly went beyond earlier Chinese pronouncements, in length especially, but it need not have raised the dispute to an entirely new level. With the test-ban treaty in sight, however, Khrushchev apparently considered the time ripe for a major propaganda campaign, and believed the advantages to be derived from it would far outweigh the possible disruption of a few weak Communist parties abroad.

On June 24 *Pravda* accused the Chinese leaders of "not abiding by the agreement on ending open polemics in the Communist movement." Three days later the Soviet Government demanded the recall of three members of the Chinese Embassy in Moscow and two other Chinese residing in the U.S.S.R., charging they had distributed copies of Peking's June 14 letter which had not yet been published in the Soviet Union. The ideological talks began on schedule in Moscow on July 5 and ended fifteen days later without result—indeed without even communiqué putty to conceal the cracks. By this time, however, the cracks might properly have been termed canyons, major tourist attractions.

On July 14, 1963, *Pravda* published a four-page "Open Letter of the Central Committee of the Communist Party of the Soviet Union, to Party Organizations, to all Communists of the Soviet Union," a reply to the Chinese letter of a month earlier which was also printed. Unlike the Peking communication, the Soviet Open Letter was obviously written for the man in the street. Stressing the peace theme, it accused the "Chinese comrades" of not believing "in the possibility of preventing a new world war" and of obviously underestimating "all the danger of thermonuclear war. 'The atomic bomb is a paper tiger; it is not terrible at all,' they contend." And indeed, "Some responsible Chinese leaders have also declared that it is possible to sacrifice hundred of millions of people in war."

Referring to criticism of Soviet policy during the Cuban crisis, the letter asked: "What are the Chinese leaders dissatisfied with? Is it, perhaps, the fact that it was possible to prevent the invasion of Cuba and the unleashing of a world war?" At the height of the crisis, Peking "assumed the stand of a critic," and instead of suggesting practical measures, "the Chinese leaders obviously endeavored to aggravate the situation in the Caribbean Sea area, which was tense even without this added fuel to the smoldering fire of the conflict." All in all, the leaders of the Chinese Communist Party even gave the impression of wishing to maintain and increase international tension, "especially in the relations between the U.S.S.R. and the U.S.," and they "apparently hold that the

Soviet Union should reply to provocations with provocations
. . . accept the challenge of the imperialists to a competition in
adventurism and aggressiveness; that is competition not for
insuring peace but for unleashing war."

A second major theme was Khrushchev's denunciation of
Stalin's terror. The Chinese leaders, the letter charged, "took
upon themselves the role of the defenders of the personality
cult, the propagators of Stalin's faulty ideas." The Soviet
Central Committee, "headed by Comrade Nikita Khrushchev," displayed "courage" and "boldness . . . truly Leninist
firmness of principle . . . in the struggle against the consequences of the personality cult." And the "atmosphere of fear,
suspicion and uncertainty" of that period "is gone, never to
return. . . . ask thousands upon thousands of people who
undeservedly suffered from reprisals in the period of the personality cult and to whom freedom and good repute have
been restored . . . Ask the people whose fathers and mothers
were victims of the reprisals . . . what it means for them to
get the recognition that their fathers, mothers and brothers
were honest people and that they themselves are not outcasts
in our society."

The letter also stressed Chinese criticism of the "good life"
in the Soviet Union: "Alluding to the fact that our party pro-
claims for its task the struggle for a better life for the people,
the C.P.C. [Chinese Communist Party] leaders hint at some
sort of 'bourgeoisation' and 'degeneration' of the Soviet society. According to their logic, if a people walks in shoes made
out of rags and eats thin cabbage soup from a common bowl,
that is Communism. And if a working man lives well and
wants to live still better tomorrow—that is almost the restora-
tion of capitalism!" (Apparently an Old Russian Proverb,

"Nobody shoots Nikita Sergeyevich Santa Claus," inspired this passage.)

With the conclusion of the test-ban negotiations in Moscow, the Chinese began to launch bitter attacks on this development. The treaty "is a big fraud to fool the peoples of the world," they declared in a statement of July 31. They accused the Soviet Government of "willingly allowing U.S. imperialism to gain military superiority" and asserted that "the interests of the Soviet people have been sold out, the interests of the people of the countries in the Socialist camp . . . have been sold out and the interests of all peace-loving people of the world have been sold out." The day before *Pravda* had published a letter, signed by a number of Old Bolsheviks, denouncing the Chinese Communists as imitators of Trotsky. *Pravda* and *Izvestia* published the Chinese statement on August 4, and the same day Moscow newspapers carried a 5,000-word statement denouncing the opposition to the treaty. In a dispatch of the 3rd, Henry Tanner of the *New York Times* had mentioned the "furore with which the Soviet press reacted to the Chinese attacks on the treaty," but then wrote of "the impression here that the Soviet leaders are, in fact, delighted to be able to make this the focal point of their quarrel with the Chinese."

On August 10 TASS announced a pending visit by Khrushchev to Yugoslavia, for a number of years the main target of Peking's wrath. The Soviet Premier began the well-publicized trip on the 20th, and flew back to Moscow on September 3. As mentioned earlier, these trips abroad furnish an excuse for a great deal of publicity and in circumstances unlikely to arouse suspicions of a propaganda build-up or "personality cult."

An article in *Izvestia,* the official government daily, on August 23 compared the leaders of the Peking regime to such aggressors as Genghis Khan, Napoleon, and Hitler. And the next day the same paper emphasized food shortages in China, while *Pravda* printed a whole page of anti-Chinese letters from readers. By the end of the month it was clear that a major propaganda campaign was in full swing. Many of the articles, wrote Henry Tanner on the 26th, evidently sought to discredit the Chinese abroad, but "others appear to be designed primarily for home consumption." "Each day's crop of thousands of words," he concluded, "contains only a few sentences that are not a variation of what has been said before." By this time it was also apparent that Soviet authorities were exercising restraint in their usual anti-American propaganda. While such restraint was in a sense a corollary of the anti-Peking effort, the campaign may simply have demanded most of the available newspaper and journal space.

Max Frankel, the *New York Times*'s diplomatic correspondent in Washington and for several years that paper's correspondent in Russia, paid a return visit during the summer of 1963. Observers in Moscow, he wrote from the Soviet captial on August 13, "tend to agree that the . . . Premier is somewhere near the peak of his popularity after having come through a year of severe trial." Despite the Cuban crisis, economic troubles, and intransigence on the part of Soviet intellectuals, "Mr. Khrushchev seems to rank higher than before in the popular mind, and his name remains closely linked with hopes for peace and progress. This image seems to have been sharpened by the test ban agreement and by the current Soviet line that the Chinese leaders oppose him because they advocate terror, austerity and war." Very real differences have grown up between Peking and Moscow, even greater than those existing between Yugoslavia and the U.S.S.R. at the time of Stalin's death. Nevertheless, if Mao Tse-tung hadn't existed, Nikita Sergeyevich would probably have invented him.

Reports of a below-average grain harvest, in the eastern or "virgin lands" territory especially, began to seep out of Russia at the end of August 1963. On August 30 the Canadian Government announced the sale of 300,000 tons of wheat to the U.S.S.R., and a Soviet trade delegation arrived in Ottawa early in September. As early as the 13th press reports spoke of a very large purchase as imminent, and three days later the Canadian Ministry of Trade and Commerce concluded an agreement to sell wheat and flour worth almost 500 million dollars, all of it to be delivered within a year. In mid-September West German millers signed contracts to supply 250,000 tons of flour; although bread remained plentiful, hardly any flour was available in Moscow stores at the end of September. And in a speech published on September 30, Khrushchev admitted that the poor harvest had placed the Soviet Union in a "difficult position." Australia had also sold a large quantity of wheat to Russia, and by early October only the United States still had a large exportable surplus.

For several years Japan and West European countries had been selling the U.S.S.R. large-diameter pipe for oil pipelines. But in November 1962, shortly after the Cuban crisis, the N.A.T.O. Council, at the insistence of the United States, recommended an embargo on such exports. And in March 1963 the West German Government forced several Ruhr companies to cancel contracts for 163,000 tons of pipe. Germany, declared Chancellor Adenauer, was honor bound to respect the N.A.T.O. decision. German business men argued, however, that Moscow would place the orders elsewhere, and in the face of this argument the Chancellor had to resort to a parliamentary maneuver to force through the cancellation order. Although Italy and Japan were reluctantly maintaining the embargo, in Bonn on May 17 the German Foreign Minister lodged a vigorous protest with the British Ambassador over the impending sale of pipe by a British firm.

But the situation was somewhat different in the United States, especially after the Cuban crisis had been forgotten. While the farm vote may not be as important as it once was, it still commands much greater respect than the pipe-manufacturer's vote. Thus in Washington on September 16, Senator Hubert H. Humphrey, the Democratic whip, declared that wheat was not a war material and called for a change in "outdated" export policies to assure the United States its share in the world market. In Iowa two days later, farmers asked the visiting Secretary of Agriculture, Orville L. Freeman, about American wheat sales to Russia. "I think we ought to sell to them," replied Mr. Freeman, "if they're willing to pay our price." And the next day the press was reporting as imminent a formal Soviet approach in Washington.

But the United States made the approach. Early in October Llewellyn Thompson was instructed to sound out Soviet Ambassador Dobrynin. The reply came on October 5: Moscow was indeed interested in buying grain at the world market price, and it could be shipped in American vessels. President Kennedy conferred on the 7th with officials concerned with such a sale; the same day William Blair of the *New York Times* reported "administration officials" as having "said today the President would probably announce his ap-

proval tomorrow or on Wednesday at his news conference."
And as predicted, on Wednesday, October 9, the President
announced his decision, "that such sales by private dealers
for American dollars or gold, either cash on delivery or normal commercial terms, should not be prohibited by the Government."[7]

In February 1963 the U.S. Air Force had reportedly dis-
continued low-level reconnaissance sorties over Cuba, but
the administration made no effort to curb anti-Castro *émigré*
groups. During the night of March 17, a launch approached
a Cuban port from the sea and opened fire with a heavy machine gun on the Soviet freighter *Lgov*. Ten days later the
Soviet freighter *Baku* was the object of a similar night-time
attack. The same day the Soviet Foreign Ministry made a
formal protest to the U.S. Embassy regarding the first attack,
and the next day (March 28) an unidentified jet fired bursts
near an American ship in international waters off Cuba. The
Soviet Foreign Ministry delivered a stiffer protest on the 29th,
warning that the Soviet Government "cannot ignore these
provocations" and was considering "appropriate measures to
ensure the security of Soviet merchant ships."

In Washington the following day, March 30, the State and
Justice Departments issued a statement: "These attacks are
neither supported nor condoned by this Government" which
would "take every step necessary to insure that such raids
are not launched, manned or equipped on United States territory." And while the United States sympathized with the
Cuban *émigrés*, it was not prepared "to see our own laws vio-
lated with impunity or to tolerate activities which might provoke armed reprisals, the brunt of which would be borne by
the armed forces of the United States." President Kennedy

also referred to the matter during his press conference on April 3: The raids, he said, give "additional incentives for the Soviet Union to maintain their personnel in Cuba; to send additional units to protect their merchant ships." Continued attacks, warned the President, "will bring reprisals, possibly on American ships. We will then be expected to take a military action to protect our ships. It may bring a counter-action. . . . issues of war and peace hang in the balance."[8] Although Stalin, who had no atom bombs at the time, may have had similar qualms regarding the 1946–49 attacks on Greece from Communist Albania, Yugoslavia, and Bulgaria, he didn't voice them publicly.

On March 31 the Department of Justice restricted some eighteen to twenty-five anti-Castro Cubans to the Miami, Florida, area. The same day customs agents in Miami seized a private yacht which was being prepared for a raid on Cuba, and in the Bahamas British authorities arrested seventeen members of an anti-Castro group and seized their heavily armed launch. And in Washington on April 5 the Coast Guard announced the dispatch of six additional planes and twelve patrol boats to the Florida-Puerto Rico area. The reinforcements, said the announcement, would aid in enforcing the laws applying to "Cuba-bound raiding vessels" and in apprehending "persons suspected of aggressive intentions against Cuba."

On March 31 a senior British official had flown to Berlin in a private plane without incident, and according to an April 1 press dispatch from the city U.S. authorities considered the situation there quieter than it had been for a long time. No trouble worth mentioning had occurred for months, and traffic to the West was being allowed to move freely. The next day, however, a Soviet fighter fired bursts near a private plane piloted by Hughie Greene, a star of British television. Mr. Greene ignored signals to land and reached Berlin safely. At the Air Safety Center on the 4th, a Soviet representative protested the flight as a "misuse of the air corridors" and stated that the U.S.S.R. would not "guarantee the safety of such flights to and from West Berlin in the future." But the next day Soviet authorities adopted a more moderate stand, and on the 6th Mr. Greene flew the plane out of Berlin without incident. Allied officials claimed a firm stand had forced the Russians to back down. From Moscow on April 10, however, Seymour Topping reported new Soviet interest in talks on Berlin "after a period of a month in which they appeared content to accept the status quo." And on the 26th a Soviet jet flew close (within 1,500 feet) to two U.S. Army helicopters over Berlin but not close enough to provoke a protest.

The underground nuclear tests in Nevada had been canceled on May 13, and a few days later East German guards began to delay weekend civilian traffic on the Berlin autobahn, checking papers, etc., with deliberate slowness. Then on May 19, when the convoy commander refused to order his men to dismount for a head count, Soviet officers held up a Berlin-bound U.S. Army convoy of twenty-two vehicles and seventy men for almost four hours. A week-long slowdown of civilian traffic occurred at the beginning of June, and East-zone police also seized a West German journalist on the autobahn. President Kennedy delivered his conciliatory American University speech on June 10, and the next day part of an American convoy was delayed for more than an hour on its way to Berlin, again because the officer in charge refused to order his men out of their trucks for a count.

The Cuban crisis undoubtedly had a very salutary, sobering effect upon Nikita Sergeyevich. But then the American crackdown on the Cuban exiles at the end of March 1963 and President Kennedy's subsequent eagerness to secure the test-ban treaty evidently caused him to reconsider his conclusions of October and November 1962. He may have begun to suspect that the President's vigorous reaction in October, occurring as it did on the eve of the mid-term elections in the United States, was an act of political desperation rather than statesmanlike determination. During the spring of 1963, however, the firm stand of American officers in West Berlin offered no confirmation of this suspicion, and by the end of June the "Perils of Peking" and "Terminated Terrors of Testing" shows were almost ready for the "peaceful coexistence" circuit. Aware that he couldn't wear his halo and have horns in it too, Nikita Sergeyevich apparently decided against further probes for the time being.

But on September 21 *Izvestia* published a statement which, while attacking the Peking regime, called for an end to "open polemics . . . because they only stir up and deepen disagreement." And Khrushchev made a similar remark to a group of visiting left-wing journalists on October 25: The wisest thing, he said, "would be to stop the polemics" and let time "say its word on which point is the more correct." The existing differences, he warned, "are like balm for the enemies of Communism . . . Why should they be given that satisfaction and why should the friends of peace and Socialism be grieved?"[9] Of course Nikita Sergeyevich may have been displaying an ostensibly conciliatory attitude merely to throw the blame for a final break on the Chinese. But by the beginning of November the Communist regime in Poland also seemed to be seeking to smooth over the dispute. And in mid-November Hungarian journalists were instructed to avoid direct reference to the Moscow-Peking conflict. During the second half of November and during December, statements in the Soviet press and unofficial reports indicated continued efforts to end or at least reduce the wrangling, and on December 26, Mao's birthday, Khrushchev sent a congratulatory message in which he addressed the Chinese leader as "comrade." Although his overtures were rejected, it is clear that by the autumn of 1963 Nikita Sergeyevich felt the "Perils of Peking" show had served its purpose.

A planned reduction (600 men) of the U.S. garrison in Berlin was disclosed in mid-September, and from the city on September 26 Arthur Olsen of the *New York Times* reported "what seems to be the aimless harassment of civilian traffic" and for some autobahn travelers "waits of up to six hours." In Washington the next day the Defense Department announced plans to withdraw 5,400 line-of-communications troops from Europe. And on the 30th in Bonn it was disclosed that withdrawal of an armored cavalry regiment and eventually a total of 40,000 troops from West Germany had been contemplated. According to the information given Arthur Olsen, the plan was abandoned only when Dr. Gerhard Schröder, the West German Foreign Minister, appealed directly to President Kennedy. And East-zone guards delayed civilian traffic on the autobahn for approximately three hours on October 5.

Although President Kennedy made the formal announcement only on the 9th, by the evening of October 7 administration approval of the wheat sales seemed assured. And at 9:00 A.M., local time, October 10, when the convoy commander refused to order his troops to dismount, Soviet officers at the Marienborn (western end) autobahn check point halted a U.S. Army convoy of sixty-one men on eighteen vehicles en route to Berlin. At 11:25 that night, the convoy commander, 1st Lt. Raymond C. Fields, acting on orders, moved his vehicles to block all east-bound traffic; another American convoy bound for West Germany, which had also been halted, did the same in the opposite lane. The orders of the Soviet officer in charge at the check point evidently didn't cover this unexpected move, and he cleared the Berlin-bound convoy at 12:15 A.M. on the 11th and the other one forty-five minutes later.

When it arrived at the Babelsberg check point just outside West Berlin at 4:00 A.M., however, the east-bound convoy was again halted. Shortly before noon, again acting on orders, Lieutenant Fields attempted to move his convoy through without clearance, but had to halt when the Soviet officer in charge blocked the road with two armored personnel carriers. The day before President Kennedy had raised the matter with Soviet Foreign Minister Gromyko who was in Washington at the time. Secretary of State Rusk also protested to Ambassador Dobrynin, and on the 11th the British, French, and West German ambassadors were summoned for morning and afternoon meetings. The same day President Kennedy met for an hour at noon and a half hour late in the afternoon with Secretary Rusk, Defense Secretary McNamara, and Llewellyn E. Thompson, the former ambassador to Moscow. According to an October 12 press report from Berlin, "Soviet authorities had been warned of appropriate countermeasures." And as Arthur Olsen reported from Bonn on the 13th, "It is believed that the next planned move—in

Berlin but not necessarily at the scene of the stoppage—was imminent when the convoy was abruptly freed"—at 12:46 P.M., October 12, and on American terms: the troops had not dismounted. At Babelsburg on the 16th, Soviet officers halted a British Army convoy of nine trucks and twenty-eight men, but cleared it on Western terms, i.e. the troops did not dismount, at 3:30 P.M. after a delay of nine hours.

As White House press secretary Salinger said during the October 10–12 incident, "the events speak for themselves," but apparently no one in the administration wished to listen. President Kennedy and his advisers, reported Max Frankel on the 12th, "concluded today" that the blockade of the U.S. convoy "was caused by a Soviet misunderstanding rather than by provocation." Washington sources, he continued, "did not expect the brief flare-up to interfere with plans to permit the sale of at least $250 million in wheat to the Soviet Union. They said that would happen only if a series of other incidents produced new international as well as domestic political pressures on the White House." In Congress Senator Thomas J. Dodd later (November 5) denied the theory that an overzealous Soviet officer had provoked the incident: "Such orders come from the highest authority in the Kremlin. Yet we sit by like boobs and make excuses for their ruthless, inexcusable conduct toward us."

At the University of Maine on October 19, President Kennedy delivered a speech on relations with the Soviet Union. Mild, fair, and reasonable, the address was ideally designed to express good will but not, alas, to impress the Soviet Premier. American policy, said the President, is directed at "convincing the Soviet leaders that it is dangerous for them to engage in direct or indirect aggression"—and then he proceeded to give the impression that it might be fairly safe after all. President Kennedy defended the test-ban treaty and the decision to sell wheat: Without making these moves, he said, "we could never, in case of war, satisfy our own hearts and minds that we had done all that could be done to avoid the holocaust of endless death and destruction." Any Communist leader might reasonably conclude that Kennedy would take further steps to avoid "endless death and destruction." The American Eagle, said the President in his concluding remarks, "still faces toward the olive branch of peace."[10]

In Chicago the same day, Deputy Defense Secretary Gilpatric was also making a speech—about a "series of evolutionary changes in the composition and disposition of military units stationed overseas." But any troop withdrawals from Europe, he said, "so far as possible," would be in line with agreed N.A.T.O. policies. And a report from Washington on October 21 (by John W. Finney of the *New York Times*) spoke of the withdrawal of some tactical air units from Britain, France, and Spain in 1964; after 1965 "Pentagon leaders are not excluding the possibility of withdrawal of one or more divisions from West Germany. In fact, they are strongly suggesting it." By this time reports were appearing of West German fears that a troop cut might in fact be imminent. Secretary Rusk apparently allayed these fears, however, in talks with West German leaders in Bonn. "There exists complete agreement on all questions of defense policy," declared the West German Defense Ministry on the 25th. And in a speech in Frankfurt on the 27th, the Secretary of State publicly denied the rumors of troop withdrawals.

But a quite credible report from Paris on October 30 (by Jack Raymond of the *New York Times*) charged that the 2nd

Battle Group of the 26th Infantry, 1,800 men, had already returned to the United States. The U.S. European Command Headquarters "was forbidden to announce the return of these troops," and another battle group was to be withdrawn in January. While these shifts were part of a regular rotation of units, "there is some doubt, however, whether the rotation will continue." And in addition an armored cavalry regiment of some 5,000 men was also scheduled to return to the United States. In Washington the same day a Defense Department spokesman stated merely that he could not confirm the plan to withdraw the cavalry regiment.

In Washington the next day, October 31, the first question at President Kennedy's press conference referred to the reports of troop withdrawals from Germany. In reply the President mentioned the additional units sent to Germany during the 1961 crisis; "we are prepared to keep these additional combat units in Germany as long as there is a need for them," and "we are not planning any reduction in United States combat units in Germany. . . . we intend to keep our combat forces in Germany as they are today, and that's more than six combat divisions." The President admitted, however, that "we are planning some reduction in noncombat personnel." To the people in the Kremlin it may well have seemed that the United States had indeed been planning to withdraw significant forces from Germany and had abandoned the idea only because of a probably adverse public reaction.

Yet another development at this time may have been interpreted in Moscow as a sign of weakness. During the 1961 Berlin crisis, one American convoy commander, having no instructions to the contrary and wishing to have his trucks cleared as quickly as possible, acceded to a Soviet request and ordered his men to dismount for a head count. And once granted, of course, Soviet authorities repeatedly demanded this concession on subsequent occasions. While not announcing it, the U.S. Army adopted a policy of allowing thirty or more troops to dismount, not including drivers and assistant drivers in the front seat. According to one account, this policy had been disclosed informally to the Russians as early as the October 10–12 incident. And the three allied powers formally communicated their procedures to Soviet military authorities on October 29.

Having informed the Russians, the allied commands in Germany decided to find out if their policies would be recognized. An American convoy of twelve vehicles and forty-four men rolled up to the Marienborn check point on its way to Berlin at 9:00 A.M., November 4. Soviet officers at first demanded that the troops dismount; when this demand was refused, they then asked that the tail gates of the trucks be lowered; when this was also refused they asked, in vain, that the men stand up in the trucks for a count. Apparently Nikita Sergeyevich was willing to settle for a very thin slice of salami. The Soviet officer in charge refused clearance, and after waiting until almost midnight, the convoy commander attempted to move ahead on his own. Three Soviet armored personnel carriers then parked across the highway, and later other Soviet armored vehicles were moved behind and alongside the trucks.

Although the Department of Commerce had issued as early as October 23 an export license for almost two million dollars' worth of corn for Hungary, the first wheat was sold to the U.S.S.R. only on January 3, 1964—and the first shipload sailed, from Norfolk, Virginia, only on January 29. On November 5, while the convoy was still waiting at Marienborn,

Senator Thomas J. Dodd introduced in the Senate a resolution expressing Congressional disapproval of any wheat sales until the Soviet Government had agreed to concessions on Allied access to Berlin. As Senator Dodd pointed out, "we sit at the conference table with them to negotiate the sale of wheat which they desperately require. . . . apparently disregarding new and deliberate acts of Soviet aggression . . . For all this, we have only ourselves to blame."

During the afternoon of the 5th the French, British, and West German ambassadors conferred at the State Department, and that evening President Kennedy met with Secretary Rusk, Defense Secretary McNamara, and others. After the meeting, Soviet Ambassador Dobrynin spoke with Mr. Rusk and presumably informed him the convoy would be allowed to proceed. "The envoy," wrote Henry Raymont of the *New York Times,* "was reported eager to dispel any fear here that the incident represented a hardening of Soviet policy that might, in turn, endanger negotiations now under way for the sale of American wheat to the Soviet Union."[11] At 10:00 P.M. a west-bound French convoy was cleared at Marienborn without difficulty and at 11:15 a British convoy. By midnight, 7:00 P.M. Washington time, there were signs at Marienborn that the American vehicles would also be allowed to proceed. The convoy commander, however, refused to permit routine processing until the Soviet armor had been removed, and the trucks were not able to move out until a few minutes after 2:00 A.M., November 6.

In Moscow at 7:25 P.M., October 31—after the mild American statements of mid-October and after the reports of troop cuts, but before the second autobahn incident—Soviet security police arrested a visiting Yale Professor, Frederick C. Barghoorn, on charges of espionage. Since Professor Barghoorn had been planning to leave for Warsaw the next day, the affair became known only on November 12 when the Soviet Foreign Ministry informed the U.S. Embassy.

News of the arrest aroused a storm of protest in the United States, especially in academic and liberal circles. At the Presidential news conference on November 14, a reporter asked, "what do you say to those Americans who say that in such a situation we should not sell wheat to the Soviet Union?" In reply the President (mistakenly?) cited the availability of wheat from other sources, Australia and Canada, and expressed doubt "that the wheat can carry other loads." But, he continued, "quite obviously this kind of trade depends upon a reasonable atmosphere in both countries. I think that atmosphere has been badly damaged by the Barghoorn arrest. . . . Professor Barghoorn I regard as a very serious matter."

While the Soviet Government apparently intended to pay cash for the wheat (1963 record gold sales abroad were estimated at over 400 tons), it was also planning a very large expansion of the chemical and fertilizer industry. And as Khrushchev later indicated (speeches to Central Committee on December 9 and 13), he hoped for Western credits to help finance this program. In mid-November the Senate was considering an amendment to the foreign aid bill which would prohibit any U.S. Government guarantees of credits to Communist countries. As President Kennedy emphasized privately in a November 15 letter to Senator Mike Mansfield, such an amendment "would jeopardize not only the projected sale of wheat to the Soviet Union, but possible sales of other important quantities of other products."[12] Apparently the Soviet Premier was thinking along the same lines (a credit restriction was finally defeated in Congress only on December 24), for at noon on November 16 Foreign Minister Gromyko informed the U.S. chargé that Professor Barghoorn would be released, and four hours later Soviet police placed him aboard a London-bound airliner.

Encouraged by President Kennedy's conciliatory attitude, the Soviet Premier was beginning to recover from the shock of the Cuban crisis by the spring of 1963. By fall, after the Sino-Soviet name calling and test-ban Novocain had time to take effect, he evidently considered it safe enough to provoke the autobahn incidents and arrest Professor Barghoorn. The United States, said Nikita Sergeyevich shortly after the Cuban affair, may be a paper tiger but it has atomic teeth. With his moves in the fall of 1963, he was attempting to demonstrate that the teeth weren't too dangerous after all since the United States also had a tissue-paper President who would allow the tiger to be snipped away a little bit at a time. Even after the clear Soviet back-down at the end of the second autobahn incident, Khrushchev attempted to give the impression that the United States had weakened. The convoy, he told a group of visiting American industrialists in Moscow on November 6, "made an attempt to ignore the established procedure. Thus our armored trucks came out of concealment to bar the way and then the Americans and British agreed to observe the established procedure." At the United Nations the same day a Soviet representative denied the accuracy of American press reports of the incident. The British, French, and U.S. convoys had all complied with standard Soviet procedures, he declared. In Washington the next day, however, Secretary of State Rusk assured reporters that the United States had not retreated an inch, "Our convoy went through in exact accordance with procedures that have been in effect a long time."

This was the situation on November 22, 1963 when Lyndon B. Johnson, an unknown and rather ominous quantity for the Kremlin, succeeded the assassinated John F. Kennedy. Soviet representatives in Britain, reported the *New York Time*'s Sydney Gruson from London six days later, had privately expressed their fears "that the Communist background of Lee H. Oswald, who was charged with the killing of President Kennedy, may be exploited in the United States to produce a harsh anti-Russian atmosphere." On November 30 in Washington, Ambassador Dobrynin turned over to the State Department the Soviet consular and other files dealing with Oswald's residence in the U.S.S.R. and his applications for visas. Officials in Washington could recall no similar instance in which the Soviet Government had shown such eagerness to cooperate. This action, wrote Jack Raymond, "appeared to reflect Kremlin concern lest reports that Oswald had identified himself as a 'Marxist,' and the fact that he had a Russian wife and other Soviet links, might place the Soviet Union in an unfavorable light in American public opinion."

Shortly after President Kennedy's death, Pierre Salinger, who had retained his post as Presidential press secretary, received an urgent invitation to lunch with a high official of the Soviet Embassy. "The Chairman [Khrushchev] has asked me to see you," said the Russian, once they were seated at the table. "He knows you and he trusts you, and he would like your estimate of the new President of the United States." President Johnson, replied the press secretary, wanted peace and good relations with the Soviet Union just as much as Kennedy had.[13] And at a Finnish Embassy dinner in Moscow on December 3, apparently the first occasion to offer itself, the Soviet Premier went out of his way to make several friendly remarks about President Johnson. "While the Soviet leaders," reported Henry Tanner, "did not appear to expect any basic changes in United States foreign policy, it was unmistakable that during the first days following President Kennedy's death they had felt some anxiety about the future of United States-Soviet relations."

On November 29 the Soviet Embassy in The Hague had announced the decision to release two Netherlands citizens who had been arrested in the U.S.S.R. in 1961 on charges of espionage and were serving thirteen-year sentences. (Presumably the supply of American political convicts in Soviet prison camps was exhausted.) And on December 5 the East-zone regime indicated to West Berlin authorities its willingness to grant Christmas-holiday passes for visits to the Eastern sector of the city. After some negotiation, passes were indeed issued; between December 19 and January 6, 1964, one and a quarter million West Berliners were allowed through the wall to visit relatives.

At this point the temptation to quote a final Old Russian Proverb is irresistible, one that fits Khrushchev's 1963 maneuvers as though coined for him

> When the Devil was sick,
> The Devil a saint would be.

Since the departure of Nikita Sergeyevich, we have experienced a lull similar to the post-Stalin lull of 1953–60; i.e. the regime has tried to maintain its international position, but no one has had enough authority at home to launch bold new ventures abroad. Sooner or later, however, once Khrushchev's eventual successor bluffs and bites his way to the head of the pack, the second part of the "proverb" will apply:

> When the Devil was well,
> The devil a saint was he.

9

Why Suffer for Saigon?
— or Die for Danzig?

Maxim Litvinov, People's Commissar of Foreign Affairs of the U.S.S.R. from 1930 until 1939 and Soviet Ambassador to Washington for several years during World War II, was perhaps one of the ablest of those who have influenced Russia's foreign policy since the Revolution. Although retired a short time later, in 1946, when Walter Bedell Smith arrived in Moscow as U.S. Ambassador, Litvinov was still serving obscurely as one of Molotov's deputies in the Foreign Ministry, and Ambassador Smith was able to obtain an interview—"the most remarkable conversation I ever had with a Soviet official."

Relations between the two countries were already beginning to deteriorate, and the ambassador asked if they might not improve again with the passage of time as younger men assumed the guidance of Soviet foreign affairs. Litvinov, who spoke English and required no interpreter, expressed himself in a burst of desperate frankness: "How could that be," he replied, "when the young men are moulded exactly in the same pattern as the old?" For a time during the war, he had believed real postwar cooperation might be possible, "but wrong decisions have been made by people who know little about the world outside the Soviet Union," and he saw "nothing better before us but a prolonged period of armed truce."[1]

Litvinov spoke with some justice, but the pattern has changed slightly. The Old Bolsheviks were hunted criminals. Those who spent most of their lives in Russia knew only two powers: the revolutionary underground and the tsarist police. Seizing power, they brought this *they-us* mentality with them and projected their image of power relationships upon the outside world.

With three or more approximately equal powers, a balance of power operates almost automatically. If power *A* becomes too powerful and dangerous, powers *B* and *C* combine against it. Should power *B* become too powerful, *A* and *C* form an alliance. But the Bolsheviks saw themselves winning everything or nothing. They perceived only two powers: the Soviet Union and an implacably hostile capitalist world. "Since the foundation of the Soviet Republics," declared that Soviet Constitution of 1923, "the States of the world have been divided into two camps: the camp of Capitalism and the camp of Socialism." As long as the capitalists didn't unite in a crusade against the U.S.S.R., what matter if one capitalist state became more powerful than the others or even brought some of them under its sway. Once Hitler had conquered France in the summer of 1940, the Soviet Union was in mortal peril. But Stalin realized the full extent of the danger only when the Germans attacked Russia in June 1941.

Until his death, Stalin continued to regard the "neutralist" countries as firmly in the capitalist "camp" and nothing more than accomplices of the United States. Khrushchev, however, joined the Communist Party when it was already in power, and the *they-us* outlook never afflicted or at least never blinded him. Thus he made a determined and not altogether unsuccessful efforts to woo these uncommitted states. And the conflict with Peking must have finally erased the last vestiges of the bipolar concept of international relations.

To a certain extent, domestic political considerations have dictated the somewhat different positions held by Soviet and Chinese Communists on relations with the capitalist world. Seeking popular approval, Khrushchev preached peaceful coexistence. Mao, on the other hand, was firmly in power and didn't need popular approval. Nevertheless, a basic difference in outlook exists. Like Lenin, Stalin, and Molotov, Mao spent much of his adult life (1927–49) in a two-power struggle: Communists versus Kuomintang. As with the Old Bolsheviks, these earlier experiences must have strongly colored his conception of Communist China's foreign relations.

Although Khrushchev apparently had a more realistic and sane view of the outside world than Stalin or Mao, the Berlin and Cuban crises demonstrated how wrong it was to consider him completely housebroken. And Soviet efforts to stir up as much trouble as possible in the Middle East without seriously involving the U.S.S.R. also reflect the Old Bolshevik tradition and are scarcely in accordance with Russian national interests.

In the long run, and not such a long run at that, enlightened self-interest governs the relations between sovereign states. Governments which base their foreign policy on anything else invite disappointment and even disaster. One of the basic policies of a great power should be to inspire trust

and confidence abroad. Sooner or later, Russian national interests will demand close cooperation with one or more capitalist powers. But if the Soviet Union's past conduct has
failed to inspire confidence, such cooperation may not be
forthcoming. In the thirties, for example, although it was
certainly not the decisive factor in the policy of appeasement
followed by the French and British governments, justified
suspicion of Soviet motives nullified much of the Kremlin's
effort to muster opposition to Hitler.

For its part, the United States should respect legitimate
Russian (not necessarily Soviet) national interests. It should
also welcome compromises and adjustments which weaken
neither country significantly and do not infringe upon the
rights and interests of third parties. The Austrian State
Treaty is a good example. But extensive, unilateral concessions on the part of Washington will inevitably put the
United States in the position in which France found herself
in August 1939, after Hitler's occupation of the Rheinland in
1936, *Anschluss* with Austria in March 1938, extortion of the
Sudetenland in the fall of that year, and occupation of the
Czech lands in March 1939.

On August 22, 1939, after Nazi Foreign Minister Ribbentrop's trip to Moscow had been announced, William Bullitt,
the U.S. Ambassador to Paris, spoke with the French Premier.
"Daladier said to me this afternoon," reported the ambassador,

that the action of the Soviet Government in signing a non-aggres-
sion pact with Germany, the secret clauses of which were unknown, placed France in a most tragic and terrible situation. . . .
he was faced with the alternative of sacrificing the lives of all
able-bodied men in France in a war, the outcome of which would

be to say the least doubtful; or the worse alternative of abandoning the commitments of France to support Poland which would
be a horrible moral blow to the French people and would result
in Germany swallowing one after another, Poland, Rumania,
Hungary, Yugoslavia, Bulgaria, Greece and Turkey. In the end
Germany would turn on France and England with all the economic resources of these countries at her disposal.[2]

A surrender or even a major concession on Berlin or elsewhere would certainly produce dangerous repercussions
among neutrals and among the allies of the United States—
anxious glances at the Communist band wagon and efforts to
reserve seats on it at the very least. But the effect on any Soviet leader could be far worse. Such a development might
cause him to succumb to the occupational disease of dictators—overconfidence.

Stalin suffered from it repeatedly after 1939. Although desiring a pact with Hitler above all else in that year, he feared
a Nazi trick and made his feelers with extreme caution. The
pact itself and the subsequent "correct" German attitude
during the 1939/40 Soviet-Finnish Winter War, and when
Moscow seized the Baltic States and parts of Rumania in the
summer of 1940, apparently made Stalin so overconfident
that the 1941 German attack on the U.S.S.R. came as a great
shock. According to Khrushchev, Stalin cried out in despair
that they had lost everything Lenin had won, all that had
been achieved since 1917.

After the war the success of Soviet moves in Eastern Europe, and especially the coup in Czechoslovakia, produced a
new accession of overconfidence. Stalin thought to topple
Tito with nothing more than a propaganda blast: "I will
shake my little finger and there will be no more Tito," he re-

marked to Khrushchev in 1948.[3] Although sobered somewhat by the failure of the Berlin blockade, Stalin felt a North Korean attack on South Korea would produce no U.S. reaction, especially after the Soviet Union exploded its first atomic bomb in 1949 and after the United States disavowed any intention of protecting the country. Some evidence indicates that the prompt American military intervention in this instance also came as something of a shock.

This peculiarity of Stalin's foreign policy may be attributed to the personal dread he inspired after the *Yezhovshchina*, the Great Purge of 1937–38. In 1939 none of the surviving competent Soviet diplomats and senior Red Army officers dared oppose the pact with Hitler, although some of them must have seen the dangers clearly. (Shaposhnikov, the Chief of Staff and a general staff officer under the Tsar, can hardly have been blinded by the Old Bolshevik *they-us* outlook.) After the German victory over France, no one dared point out that Hitler was now in a position to attack the U.S.S.R. with all his forces; such a warning would have contained the implication that Stalin had blundered in signing the pact in 1939. If anything this atmosphere grew worse after the war and ended only with Stalin's death in 1953.

Khrushchev was never so powerful and awful that no one dared tell him any unpleasant truth. And the same will probably be true of his successors. After a few successes, however, dictators can become overconfident despite repeated warnings from their advisers. At noon on September 1, 1939, only hours after German troops had attacked Poland, Hitler spoke scornfully to Foreign Minister Ribbentrop of the warnings he had received from the professional German diplomats. They sit in every capital, he declared, and should have their finger on the pulse of the nation to which they are accredited. But what happens when I ask them for an opinion? The introduction of conscription means war, they warned. The occupation of the Rheinland means war. The *Anschluss* with Austria means war. The Sudeten crisis means war. And the occupation of Prague means war. The generals were no better. "You must understand," said Hitler, "that I finally have no further use for the advice of people who have misinformed or even lied to me a dozen times, and I prefer to rely on my own judgment which has advised me better on all these occasions than the responsible expert."

Two days later, when informed of the British declaration of war (in the form of an ultimatum), Hitler sat as though turned to stone. Finally, looking at Ribbentrop, he asked, "What now?"[4]

The peace of kings and princes established at Vienna in 1815 lasted almost a century; that of peoples established at Versailles in 1919 lasted only twenty years. This is the age of the Common Man and slogans reflecting a sound foreign policy seldom win votes. French politicians lacked the moral courage to stop Hitler in 1936 while they could still do so without a major war. And the responsible British politicians would hardly have supported them had they acted. In both countries these politicians remained in power, with some cabinet shuffling—until 1940. In the United States, even after 1940 when Britain stood alone against Nazi Germany, isolationism was a powerful force and no politician dared advocate too much support for Britain. And in 1941, only a few months before Pearl Harbor, Congress almost disbanded the conscript army authorized the year before.

Harry Truman, on the other hand, regarded the Presidency of the United States as a very responsible position. Although unable to resist the "bring the boys home" outcry in 1945, Mr. Truman acted as he thought the President of the United States should act when the chips were down in 1950 —and the next election be damned! The Democrats lost the next election, but the post-Korea peace lasted longer than that which followed World War II.

"Wishful thinking," declared Soviet Foreign Minister Shepilov in 1957, led certain persons in the West to expect "some 'evolution' of the Soviet system, to expect us to renounce 'some aspects' of the dictatorship of the proletariat and become at least 'pink' if not actually 'white.'" But these "calculations on an 'evolution' of the Soviet system toward a bourgeois regime were empty fantasy."[5]

Although Shepilov was undoubtedly correct, two years earlier, for the first time since World War II, the Soviet regime had made a meaningful concession, the Austrian State Treaty, and adopted a policy of live-and-let-live. Even if this policy was insincere and only temporary, it did produce concrete results favorable to both Russia and the West. Had the Western powers continued to maintain an unbending attitude, additional similar results might have been obtained.

But given the influence of journalistic, literary, and cocktail-party experts on American foreign policy, this was impossible. As they used to chatter wittily about Secretary of State Dulles, "I don't know whether he frightens the Russians, but he certainly frightens me." One must agree with Shepilov: With their sheltered backgrounds, their "education" consisting largely of indoctrination with the current clichés, these people regard their own wishful thinking as reality. Surrounded by persons of this sort, it was only natural for President Kennedy to adopt a conciliatory attitude toward the U.S.S.R. And with his Soviet background, Khrushchev inevitably misinterpreted this attitude as reflecting fear and weakness. The Berlin and Cuban-missile crises followed.

"I think looking back on Cuba," said the President in a television interview of December 17, 1962, "what is of concern is the fact that both governments were so far out of contact, really. I don't think that we expected that he would put the missiles in Cuba, because it would have seemed such an imprudent action for him to take, as it was later proved. Now he obviously must have thought that he could do it in secret and that the United States would accept it. So that he did not judge our intentions accurately."[6]

Laurence A. Steinhardt, the American Ambassador to the Soviet Union from 1939 until 1941, could have given President Kennedy some very good advice. "Approaches by Britain or the United States must be interpreted here as signs of weakness and the best policy to pursue is one of aloofness indicating strength," he wrote from Moscow on October 20, 1940 to a friend in the State Department.

Soviet authorities have been more recalcitrant, uncooperative, and stubborn than usual during the past three or four weeks. This is easy to explain. As long as the attitude in Washington was unfriendly, we were getting results here. As soon as the Oumansky-Welles conferences began to take shape in Washington, [Soviet Ambassador] Oumansky undoubtedly reported the same as a great personal victory . . . As you know, from your own experience, the moment these people here get it into their heads that we are "appeasing them, making up to them, or need them," they immediately stop being cooperative. . . . I assume that the "higher ups" [in Washington] regarded international "policies" as more important than profitable results and are still fooling themselves into believing that the Soviet Government responds to kindness or evidences of good will. My experience has been that they respond only to force and if force cannot be applied, then to straight oriental bartering or trading . . . That, in my opinion, is the only language they understand and the only language productive of results. It also has the advantage of gaining their respect. . . . I can imagine just what you are up against in trying to get this point of view across. It must be all the more difficult with the British and American press endeavoring to formulate our foreign policy.[7]

Steinhardt's judgment applies to relations with any Communist government, indeed to relations with any totalitarian regime. True, the Communist states no longer form a monolithic bloc as they did under Stalin, but they still have much more in common with one another than with capitalist states. The world Communist movement can no longer be compared to a massed battalion with all the parties and states stepping off on the left foot when Stalin gave the command "march." But most of them are still marching in the same general direction, even though in extended order and at different speeds. In certain situations, this in itself can lead to a more rapid and prolonged advance. World communism may not be monolithic at present, but neither were the aggressor powers of World War II—Germany, Italy, Japan, and the U.S.S.R. from 1939 until 1941. Nevertheless, the successes of one invariably encouraged the others.

That the Soviet Union refrained from any major probes in the West for several years after Khrushchev's fall may be attributed in part to President Johnson's action in sending ground combat units to Vietnam. (The existence of a collective leadership in Moscow and the growing hostility of Communist China were other inhibiting factors.) Mr. Johnson's mistake was in not intervening more quickly and in greater strength—and in not drafting college students first.

It is only human nature for the average person to take advantage of a legal opportunity to avoid the draft. In the past, the average student hasn't gone to Vietnam mainly because his middle-class parents could afford to keep him in college. But the truck drivers and factory workers, whose taxes pay most of the direct costs of the student's education, couldn't afford to send their children to college; instead their sons were drafted and sent to Vietnam. A student with any sensitivity at all must therefore have felt more than a little guilty about his situation. If he could persuade himself and others, however, that American policy in Vietnam was "immoral," even "obscene," then he felt perfectly justified in dodging the draft and letting the sons of the lower classes fight and sometimes die for him.

College students are of course among the most vociferous members of American society, and, as a class, their middle-class parents are among the most influential. Politicians whose main concern was election or re-election didn't have to keep their ears very close to the ground to hear and join in the clamor. The resulting, highly publicized controversy convinced Hanoi that, as in 1954, it could again win on the enemy's home front what it couldn't win in the field. Had the United States displayed half the resolution with which it fought World War II and the Korean War, the war in Vietnam would have been over by 1968—and at half the cost in lives and money.

Although John F. Kennedy was elected by a very thin margin, it wouldn't be fair to suggest that fear of offending his "liberal" supporters determined his attitude toward the

Soviet Union. It certainly wasn't true during the Cuban crisis. Since then, however, Lyndon Johnson has shown us what happens to a liberal President when the pigeons turn on him. The average "liberal" voter who elects the average "liberal" politician isn't much different from a sheep. Such sheep simply don't enjoy the barking of sheep dogs. They much prefer bland, simple slogans: e.g., "four feet good, two feet bad" (as in Orwell's *Animal Farm*), "I didn't Raise My Boy to Be a Soldier," "America First," "not afraid to negotiate," "get out of Vietnam," or "peace in our time" (this last paid for within two years by blood, sweat, and tears). But wolves salivate when they hear such slogans, and if those "liberal" politicians who seek his vote persist in bleating within earshot of the wolves, someday the Common Man may be very *un*common indeed—perhaps even extinct.

Chronology
Notes
Bibliography
Index

Chronology

1953

Stalin dies; armistice in Korea; riots in East Germany; Beria executed.

1954

Geneva agreements end war in Indochina and partition country.

1955

Austrian State Treaty; first post-Stalin summit.

1956

February
 Khrushchev denounces Stalin in speech to Twentieth Party Congress.

October
 Uprising in Hungary; near uprising in Poland; Suez crisis.

1957

June
 Zhukov and Khrushchev overcome "anti-Party group" (Molotov, Malenkov, and Kaganovich).

October
 4 Zhukov leaves Moscow en route to Yugoslavia.
 7 Khrushchev initiates Syrian crisis in interview with James Reston.
c. 24 Presidium of Supreme Soviet relieves Zhukov as Defense Minister.

c. 28　Central Committee of Soviet Communist Party meets to expel Zhukov from Party Presidium.

29　Liquidation of Syrian "crisis" begins.

1958

March

27　Khrushchev assumes chairmanship of Council of Ministers.

April

Soviet-Yugoslav relations deteriorate.

June

Execution of Imre Nagy and three other Hungarian leaders announced.

July

14　Coup in Iraq.

15　U.S. Marines land in Lebanon.

17　British paratroops land in Jordan; American and East German Red Cross officials agree on release of passengers and crew of U.S. helicopter.

19　Khrushchev proposes summit conference.

23　Khrushchev agrees to Security Council summit.

28　Khrushchev accuses U.S. Government of delaying summit meeting.

31–　[to August 3] Khrushchev confers with Mao Tse-tung in Peking.

August

5　Khrushchev rejects summit conference.

23　Siege of Quemoy begins.

September

4　Secretary of State Dulles warns of probable U.S. intervention to defend Quemoy.

6　Chou En-lai announces Peking is willing to resume talks

between U.S. and Chinese Ambassadors in Warsaw; Communist batteries suspend shelling of Quemoy; White House announces approval of ambassadorial talks.

7   Khrushchev vows support for Peking in message to Eisenhower.

October
c. 3   Chinese Nationalists apparently breaking Quemoy blockade.
4   First withdrawal of U.S. Army forces from Lebanon.
6   Communists abandon siege of Quemoy.
25   Last U.S. forces leave Lebanon.

November
10   Khrushchev demands end of "occupation regime in Berlin."

1959

September
Khrushchev visits United States.

1960

May
1   U-2 shot down over Soviet Union.
16   Khrushchev disrupts Paris summit by demanding apology from President Eisenhower.

July
1   Soviet fighter shoots down RB-47 over Barents Sea.
1 & 8   Khrushchev warns against Berlin session of Bundestag.

August
9   Secretary of State Herter says Bundestag session matter for Bonn to decide.
30   East German authorities begin halting West Germans en route to meetings in West Berlin.

September
8 East German regime restricts entry of West Germans into East Berlin.
30 Bonn gives notice of abrogation of trade pact with East Germany.

December
29 Bonn renews trade pact with East Germany.

1961

January
20 President Kennedy takes office.
25 Two surviving crew members of RB-47 released by Soviet Government.

April
17 Anti-Castro landing in Cuba.
18 Mob attacks U.S. Embassy in Moscow.
21 Ulbricht makes new threats regarding West Berlin.

May
c. 1 Moscow proposes summit talks.

June
3–4 Kennedy-Khrushchev talks in Vienna; Khrushchev hands over memorandum on Berlin.
8 Moscow protests planned Bundesrat session in Berlin.
15 Khrushchev announces year-end ultimatum on Berlin.
21 Khrushchev repeats ultimatum.

July
20 Soviet Ambassador Menshikov sails from New York for home.
25 President Kennedy announces new defense measures.
30 Soviet Ambassador Smirnov called home from Bonn.

August

2 Khrushchev tells Italian Premier Fanfani he favors talks on Berlin.

3 In notes to Western Allies, Soviet Government says it is prepared for talks.

3–5 Party First Secretaries of Warsaw Pact countries meet in Moscow.

7 In radio-TV address Khrushchev urges talks.

13 Communists seal off Berlin.

31 Soviet Government announces new series of nuclear tests.

September

19 Khrushchev reportedly tells Paul-Henri Spaak he will not insist on year-end deadline for German treaty.

24 Marshal Konev protests U.S. military police patrols on autobahn.

30 Soviet Foreign Minister Gromyko tells Secretary of State Rusk his government will not insist on year-end deadline.

October

15 Communist police halt four American cars attempting to enter East Berlin.

17 Khrushchev announces he will not insist on year-end deadline.

22 U.S. military police escort first auto over sector border in Berlin.

25–26 Military police escort other autos over sector border.

27 Military police again escort car over border; Soviet tanks move up to Friedrichstrasse crossing point.

28 U.S. Government retreats, orders end to escorting autos over sector border

29–30 Soviet authorities turn back U.S. military police patrols on autobahn.

November

3–4 Communist police halt U.S. Army vehicles in East Berlin.

15 East Berlin police detain British tourists and civil servants.

23 Soviet authorities detain American military passenger train.

December

8 Workmen erect customs gates at crossing points into East Berlin; Soviet officers hold up U.S. Army convoys on autobahn.

10 Rail traffic to West Berlin restricted to two tracks.

11 East-zone authorities begin delaying civilian trucks leaving West Berlin via autobahn.

23 Communist police demand identification from civilian aids accompanying General Watson on visit to Soviet headquarters in East Berlin.

1962

January

c. 1 Moscow indicates willingness to trade Powers for Abel.

15 East German authorities release two American college students.

18 Attorney General Robert Kennedy receives informal invitation to visit Moscow.

February

7 Soviet representative at Berlin air safety center makes first attempt to reserve certain altitudes in air corridors.

10 Powers and Abel exchanged in Berlin.

11 Khrushchev proposes that heads of government open disarmament conference.

14 Soviet fighters fly close to Allied planes in air corridors.

15 MIG's harrass Allied transports; Allies protest in Moscow; officials in Washington say fighters may be used as escorts, warn of counter-harassment of Communist communications.

20– [to March 11] Strong Soviet hints of new deadline on German treaty.

22 Khrushchev repeats proposals for disarmament-conference summit.

March
9 Soviet planes drop metal foil in air corridors.
12 Officials in Washington say Air Force will fly fighter escorts; General Norstad authorized to take any action considered necessary.
16 In Kremlin speech Khrushchev adopts mild tone regarding Berlin.
29 Soviet aircraft fly in air corridors for last time, harassment of Allied convoys on autobahn ends.

April
5 Marshal Konev agrees to free movement of members of U.S. military mission in East Germany.
10 Tass announces relief of Marshal Konev as Soviet commander in East Germany.
24 Gromyko tells Supreme Soviet he sees "some glimpses of hope" for agreement on Berlin.

May
15 Release of some East German troops from active duty announced.

July
2 Raul Castro arrives in Moscow with party of Cuban officers.
10 Khrushchev suggests replacement of "occupation" forces in West Berlin by U.N. troops.
17 Soviet Ambassador Dobrynin calls at White House; Soviet fighter makes pass at airliner over Germany, renewal of harassment of Berlin's air communications.
18 East-zone regime announces arrest of fifteen persons on autobahn.

21 [and 22 and 24] Secretary of State Rusk confers with Gromyko at Geneva.

23 Harassment of Western aircraft in air corridors.

26 [to August 8] Eight Soviet-bloc vessels arrive in Cuba.

31 Soviet representative warns U.S. Army helicopter may be shot down over East Berlin.

August

1 Ulbricht and Willi Stoph fly to Russia.

13 Angry demonstrations in West Berlin.

17 Communist guards shoot youth at Berlin wall and leave him to die without medical attention.

19–20 West Berlin crowds stone Soviet bus.

21 Soviet relief for memorial guards appears at Friedrichstrasse crossing in armored cars.

22 Soviet headquarters in East Berlin abolished.

23–24 U.S. Army convoys delayed on autobahn.

29 President Kennedy admits Cuban policy hampered by threat to West Berlin (press conference); Soviet antiaircraft rockets unveiled in Cuba.

September

2 Moscow admits arms aid to Cuba; Soviet authorities in Berlin instructed to use other than Friedrichstrasse crossing for relief of guards.

4 President Kennedy warns against Soviet bases or ground-to-ground missiles in Cuba; Soviet armored cars appear at Sandkrug bridge as ordered.

11 Moscow issue long statement on Cuba; says Berlin issue will not be pressed until after November elections in United States.

13 Soviet authorities instructed to use buses in Berlin; President Kennedy again warns of Cuba becoming "offensive military base" for U.S.S.R. (press conference).

14 Soviet relief appears at Sandkrug bridge in bus.

19 Soviet officers delay U.S. convoy on autobahn.

21 Civilian truck traffic delayed on autobahn.

25 Western aircraft buzzed in Berlin air corridors; Fidel Castro announces plans for port to service Soviet trawlers; Cuban Foreign Ministry forbids Western correspondents to travel outside Havana without special permission.

26 Soviet jet flies head-on at airliner in air corridor.

October

4 Washington discloses "measures" to restrict Soviet-Cuban trade.

14 U-2 pilot photographs Soviet missiles in Cuba.

16 Khrushchev calls U.S. Ambassador to Kremlin.

18 Gromyko meets with President Kennedy.

22 President Kennedy announces blockade of Cuba.

24 Blockade becomes effective; Soviet ships en route to Cuba change course.

25 Work on missile sites in Cuba proceeds.

26 Khrushchev warns he cannot keep Soviet ships immobilized at sea; sends hard-soft message to Kennedy.

27 Khrushchev makes Cuba-Turkey base exchange offer; Soviet rocket battery shoots down American U-2 over Cuba; Kennedy rejects base swap but accepts message of 26th as offer of compromise; Adlai Stevenson seeks Latin-American approval of air strike; Air Force calls up troop carrier squadrons; U.S. plane flies over Soviet territory.

28 Khrushchev agrees to withdraw surface-to-surface missiles from Cuba.

November

11 Deputy Defense Secretary Gilpatric says forty-two missiles withdrawn from Cuba, says IL-28 bombers must also go.

20 Khrushchev agrees to withdraw jet bombers from Cuba.

December

6 Department of Defense announces withdrawal of last of bombers.

12 Khrushchev addresses Supreme Soviet, makes anti-Peking remarks.

1963

January
16 Khrushchev speaks in East Berlin, condemns Albanians but calls for halt in polemics between Communist parties.

March
17 Anti-Castro raiders fire on Soviet ship in Cuban port.
27 Raiders fire on second Soviet ship, formal Soviet protest to United States.
28 Unidentified jet fires burst near American ship off Cuba.
29 Soviet Government makes stronger protest.
30 State and Justice Departments promise steps to prevent raids by Cuban exiles.

April
2 Soviet fighter fires near private plane en route to Berlin.
3 President Kennedy expresses concern over raids on Cuba.
24 British and U.S. appeals for test-ban delivered in Moscow.

May
8 Underground tests in Nevada announced.
13 Moscow radio warns against new tests; United States cancels Nevada tests.
c. 15 East German police begin to delay civilian traffic on autobahn.
19 Soviet officers delay U.S. convoy on autobahn.
31 New Anglo-American appeals for test-ban agreement.

June
6 [or 7th] Khrushchev agrees to test-ban talks in Moscow.
10 President Kennedy delivers conciliatory address at American University in Washington.
11 American convoy delayed on autobahn.
14 Chinese Communist Party sends Soviet Party lengthy letter condemning Khrushchev's policies.

July
2 Khrushchev says Soviet Government willing to ban atmospheric tests.
5 [to 20th] Sino-Soviet ideological talks in Moscow.
14 *Pravda* publishes Open Letter replying to Chinese letter of June 14.
15 Test-ban talks open in Moscow.
25 Test-ban protocol initialed.

August
5 Secretary of State Rusk signs test-ban treaty in Moscow.
20 [to September 3] Khrushchev visits Yugoslavia.

September
c. 15 [to end of month] Rumors of U.S. troop withdrawals from Germany.
16 Canada sells large quantity of wheat to U.S.S.R.
24 Senate ratifies test-ban treaty.

October
5 Civilian traffic on autobahn delayed for three hours.
7 Sale of American wheat to U.S.S.R. reported imminent.
9 President Kennedy announces approval of wheat sales.
10 [to 12th] U.S. convoy held up on autobahn.
16 British convoy delayed nine hours on autobahn.
19 President Kennedy delivers peace address at University of Maine; Deputy Defense Secretary Gilpatrick speaks of troop withdrawals from Europe.
29 Allied powers inform Soviet authorities of troop-count procedures on autoban.
30 Report of pending withdrawal of U.S. armored cavalry regiment from Germany.
31 President Kennedy denies plans to withdraw combat troops from Germany; Professor Barghoorn arrested in Moscow.

November

4 [to 6th] U.S. convoy held up on autobahn.

14 President Kennedy calls Barghoorn arrest "serious matter."

15 President Kennedy asks rejection of Senate ban on guarantees of credit to Communist countries, letter to Senator Mansfield.

16 Professor Barghoorn released.

22 Kennedy assassinated, President Johnson takes office.

29 Release of two Netherlands citizens imprisoned in Soviet Union announced.

December

5 East-zone regime offers Christmas passes to East Berlin.

Notes

CHAPTER 1

1. This exchange is reconstructed of course. Khrushchev may or may not have made the indicated reply, but on several later occasions he referred scornfully to the "arithmetical majority" mustered by the "anti-Party" group.

2. *New Leader,* Feb. 10, 1958.

3. Unless otherwise indicated, dispatches to the *New York Times* may be found in the Late City Edition of the day after the event or dispatch. All brief quotations whose sources are not given are also from the Late City Edition.

4. G. S. Franklin, *N.Y. Times Magazine,* Jan. 19, 1958.

5. *Pravda,* Jul. 4, 1957. Unless otherwise indicated, quotations of *Pravda* and *Izvestia* are from TASS translations.

6. *Pravda* and *Izvestia,* Sep. 11, 1957.

7. *Pravda* and *Izvestia,* Sep. 14, 1957.

8. *Pravda* and *Izvestia,* Oct. 16, 1957.

9. *Izvestia,* Oct. 18, 1957.

10. *Pravda* and *Izvestia,* Oct. 19, 1957.

11. *N.Y. Times,* Oct. 23, 1957.

12. Max Frankel, *N. Y. Times,* Oct. 30, 1957.

13. *Pravda* and *Izvestia,* Nov. 3, 1957.

14. *N.Y. Times,* Jun. 10, 1959.

15. *International Affairs* (monthly, Moscow), no. 11 (Nov. 1957), p. 17.

16. *Pravda* and *Izvestia,* Nov. 7, 1957.

CHAPTER 2

1. *N.Y. Times,* Jul. 16, 1958.

2. *Ibid.,* Jul. 17, 1958.

3. *Ibid.,* Jul. 19, 1958.

4. *Pravda* and *Izvestia*, Jul. 20, 1958. Dept. of State *Bulletin*, vol. 39, pp. 231–33.

5. Dept. of State *Bulletin*, vol. 39, pp. 229–31.

6. *Ibid.*, pp. 234–35.

7. *Ibid.*, pp. 233–34.

8. See *ibid.*, pp. 275–77, for an unofficial translation.

9. *Pravda*, Aug. 4; *Izvestia*, Aug. 5, 1958.

10. For an unofficial translation, see Dept. of State *Bulletin*, vol. 39, pp. 342–46.

11. Letter from Max Frankel to the author, Mar. 25, 1965. Assuming that the dispatch had indeed been cleared by the censor, the Associated Press released it with an introductory note to that effect.

12. *N.Y. Times*, Aug. 2, 1958.

13. *Pravda*, Aug. 4; *Izvestia*, Aug. 5, 1958.

14. Dept. of State *Bulletin*, vol. 39, pp. 445–46.

15. Reuters, Hong Kong, as published in the *N.Y. Times*, Sep. 7, 1958.

16. Dept. of State *Bulletin*, vol. 39, pp. 446–47.

17. See *ibid.*, pp. 499–503, for an unofficial translation.

18. Joseph Alsop had devoted a whole column (*Washington Post*, Aug. 9, 1958) to the Essoyan dispatch of August 6: "The story described the move to put the Middle East crisis into the U.N. General Assembly as Khrushchev's 'first serious diplomatic and public setback.' . . . Essoyan added that this retreat might be 'a blow to the personal fortunes of the dynamic Soviet leader.'" This was, wrote Mr. Alsop, "not a report smuggled past the Soviet censorship," and since the 1920's "Soviet censors have never permitted any foreign correspondent to send out speculation about the declining fortunes of any Soviet political leader, unless the leader's decline of fortune was already a solid, accomplished fact."

Some foreign correspondents in Moscow assumed that Mr. Essoyan had been expelled as a direct result of the Alsop column (Max Frankel, letter to the author, Mar. 25, 1965). Since a denial that Khrushchev's "decline of fortune was already a solid, accomplished fact" would have defeated its own ends by causing fresh speculation, the Kremlin denied the story indirectly by expelling Essoyan for violating censorship rules. By waiting for six weeks after the Alsop column, however, Soviet authorities were able to issue their *de facto* denial at a time when it was also useful in emphasizing Khrushchev's "determination" regarding support for China.

19. *Pravda,* Nov. 11, 1958.

CHAPTER 3

1. Stalin deliberately kept the reins of power divided, never allowing any subordinate to hold more of them than necessary. In the satellites, for example, the security policy received orders directly from the M.G.B. (now K.G.B.) in Moscow rather than from any local Party or government leader. But the death of Beria and an ensuing purge of the M.G.B. broke the top link in this chain of command, and several satellite leaders gathered the loose reins in their own hands. Nevertheless, given a general conviction that Soviet intervention need no longer be feared, the future of the regimes in Czechoslovakia, Poland, and Hungary would be uncertain to say the least, and even the situation in Rumania and Bulgaria could change.

2. Tass release in English as published in the *N.Y. Times,* May 10, 1960.

3. Tass release, Reuters, London, as published in the *N.Y. Times,* May 13, 1960. Official translation of prepared statement, Reuters, Paris, as published in the *N.Y. Times,* May 19, 1960.

4. *N.Y. Times,* Oct. 27, 1960.

5. *Ibid.,* May 17, 1960.

6. *Pravda* and *Izvestia,* May 6, 8, 1960.

7. *Pravda* and *Izvestia,* May 17, 1960.

8. *Pravda,* May 21, 1960.

CHAPTER 4

1. Arthur Bliss Lane, *I Saw Poland Betrayed* (New York: Bobbs-Merrill, 1948), pp. 311–12.

2. *N.Y. Times,* Jul. 2, 9, 1960.

3. *Neues Deutschland,* Aug. 4, 1960.

4. Dept. of State *Bulletin,* vol. 43, p. 312.

5. *Neues Deutschland,* Aug. 31, 1960.

6. *N.Y. Times,* Sep. 23, 1960.

7. *Neues Deutschland,* Dec. 18, 1960, p. 7.

8. *N.Y. Times,* Jan. 1, 21, 1961.

9. For unofficial translations see Dept. of State *Bulletin,* vol. 44, pp. 662–63.

10. *Ibid.,* p. 761.

11. For the official translation, see Dept. of State *Bulletin,* vol. 45, pp. 231–33.

12. *N.Y. Times,* Jun. 9, 1961.

13. *Pravda,* Jun. 16, 22; *Izvestia,* Jun. 17, 23, 1961.

14. *Neues Deutschland,* Jun. 28, 1961.

15. Pierre Salinger, *With Kennedy* (Garden City, N.Y.: Doubleday, 1966), p. 190.

16. *Pravda,* Aug. 8; *Izvestia,* Aug. 9, 1961.

17. *Pravda,* Aug. 31; *Izvestia,* Sep. 1, 1961.

18. *Washington Post,* Aug. 29, 1961.

19. *N.Y. Times,* Sep. 9, 1961.

20. Sydney Gruson to *N.Y. Times,* Bonn. Sep. 24, 1961.

21. *Pravda* and *Izvestia,* Oct. 18, 1961.

22. C. L. Sulzberger, "Foreign Affairs: The Two Ks and Germany," *N.Y. Times,* Nov. 6, 1966. Salinger, pp. 191–95, 198–200, 208–9, 222–37. Theodore C. Sorensen. *Kennedy* (New York: Harper and Row, 1965), pp. 552–55.

CHAPTER 5

1. *Frankfurter allgemeine Zeitung,* Aug. 19, 1961.

2. Salinger, p. 228.

3. Dept. of State *Bulletin,* vol. 46, p. 370. Most of this chapter is based on day-to-day press reports; see also Wolfgang Paul, *Kampf um Berlin* (Munich and Vienna: Albert Langen, Georg Müller Verlag, 1962), pp. 281–98.

CHAPTER 6

1. *Parliamentary Debates,* Commons, vol. 664, col. 1054.

2. *N.Y. Times,* Sep. 10, 1962.

3. *Pravda* and *Izvestia,* Jul. 11, 1962.

4. *N.Y. Times,* Jul. 13, 1962.

5. *Ibid.,* Jul. 24, 1962.

6. *Pravda* and *Izvestia,* Sep. 12, 1962.

7. *N.Y. Times,* Sep. 20, 1962.

8. *Ibid.,* Sep. 29, 1962.

9. *Ibid.,* Aug. 29, 1962.

10. *Ibid.,* Aug. 30, 1962.

11. A stronger Presidential statement at this point might conceivably have halted, temporarily at least, the shipment of medium-range missiles to Cuba. The two vessels believed to be carrying them, the *Omsk* and *Poltava,* arrived on September 8 and 15. Allowing ten days for the voyage, the first ship must have sailed from a Soviet port about August 30. And Khrushchev may have waited until September 15 or 20 before approving the shipment of jet bombers. On the 28th a U.S. Navy plane photographed crates on the deck of a Soviet freighter on its way to Cuba, crates that presumably held twin-jet IL-28's. (Roger Hilsman, *To Move a Nation*—Garden City, N.Y.: Doubleday, 1967—pp. 167, 184, 186–87.)

12. Hilsman, pp. 170–72. *Pravda,* Sep. 3, 1962.

13. *N.Y. Times,* Sep. 5, 1962.

14. *Pravda* and *Izvestia,* Sep. 12, 1962. During the first part of September, Georgi Bolshakov and Soviet Ambassador Dobrynin also made reassuring statements to Attorney General Robert Kennedy, Theodore Sorensen, and other important Presidential advisers (Robert F. Kennedy, *Thirteen Days*—New York: W. W. Norton, 1969, pp. 25–26; Sorensen, pp. 667–68; Hilsman, pp. 165–66).

15. Dept. of State *Bulletin,* vol. 47, pp. 481–82. *N.Y. Times,* Sep. 14, 1962.

16. *N.Y. Times,* Oct. 5, 1962.

17. According to an Associated Press dispatch from Havana on

September 25, the Cuban Foreign Ministry had forbidden Western correspondents to travel outside the capital without special permission. This was obviously a security precaution, and it seems safe to assume that no significant construction at the missile sites took place before this date. Nor is it improbable that large-scale construction recognizable from the air began only on or after October 5 (Hilsman, pp. 185–86).

18. Sorensen, pp. 689–91. R. F. Kennedy, pp. 39–42. Hilsman, p. 166.

CHAPTER 7

1. Hilsman, pp. 171–72, 173–76, 180. Sorensen, pp. 672–73.
2. Dept. of State *Bulletin*, vol. 47, pp. 715–20.
3. *N.Y. Times*, Oct. 24, 1962.
4. *Pravda* and *Izvestia*, Oct. 24, 1962.
5. *Pravda*, Oct. 25, 1962.
6. *Pravda*, Oct. 26; *Izvestia*, Oct. 27, 1962.
7. Hilsman, pp. 216–19. Salinger, pp. 274–76. R. F. Kennedy, pp. 87, 88–89.
8. Dept. of State *Bulletin*, vol. 47, pp. 741–43.
9. As might have been expected, Khrushchev later tried to blame this on the Chinese Communists. The U-2, said a report to the *N.Y. Times* from Warsaw on November 16, had been shot down by uniformed Chinese using Soviet rockets. The reporter cited "high Communist quarters" and "Communist circles usually not accesssible to Westerners."
10. *Washington Post*, Oct. 25, 1962. Salinger, pp. 277, 279.
11. Dept. of State *Bulletin*, vol. 47, p. 741.
12. *Ibid.*, p. 743. Salinger, pp. 277–78. Hilsman, pp. 222–23. R. F. Kennedy, pp. 107–9.
13. *N.Y. Times*, Oct. 28, 1962.
14. Dept. of State *Bulletin*, vol. 47, pp. 743–46.
15. *N.Y. Times*, Oct. 29, 1962.
16. *Ibid.*, Dec. 5, 1962.
17. *Ibid.*, Nov. 8, 1962.

18. *Neues Deutschland,* Dec. 3, 5, 1962.

19. *Pravda* and *Izvestia,* Jan. 17, 1963; translations from *Current Digest of the Soviet Press,* vol. 15, no. 3.

CHAPTER 8

1. But in Leningrad on March 13, 1964 a 24-year-old poet, Iosif Brodsky, was tried for "parasitism'" and sentenced to five years' forced labor at a "distant locality." As a Moscow lawyer later commented to an American visitor, Brodsky was not banished for "any *crime*—nothing criminal was even charged—but simply because he irritated the wrong people by living an independent life." (For a running account of the case, see the *New Leader,* August 31, September 14, and October 12, 1964.)

Several other developments in the last months of Khrushchev's rule pointed to an enhanced role for the K.G.B.: incidents at Leningrad, Tula, and Odessa involving U.S. and British service attachés, an attack (mustard-gas spray) on the anti-"bugging" technician of the German Embassy on September 6 near Moscow, a letter published in *Izvestia* the same day praising the conduct of some Cheka (security police) officers during the Stalin era, and a deliberate and outrageous violation of the diplomatic status of a group of American and British service attachés at Khabarovsk on September 28. Agents of the K.G.B. invaded the hotel rooms of the Western officers, searched their belongings, and confiscated notes and film. An account of the affair published in *Izvestia* on October 8 stressed the role of the security police: "One cannot help thinking that these 'diplomat' spies could have caused great damage to the security of the Soviet state, if our glorious Chekists had not intercepted their actions in time."

Khrushchev's son-in-law was chief editor of *Izvestia,* and older members of the Central Committee undoubtedly remembered editorials during the Great Purge of 1937–38 referring to the "iron fist of Comrade Yezhov" (then chief of the Cheka) smashing spys and fascist agents. Bitter memories of Stalin's terror and fear that it might return may not have induced the anti-Khrushchev conspirators to act but probably contributed to their success.

2. By the spring of 1964, however, Nikita Sergeyevich had apparently become overconfident and was allowing "overculting" of his personality. Between April 17 and 22, *Pravda* and *Izvestia* devoted a total of seventeen pages to Khrushchev's birthday, and *Pravda* gave him the whole front page on the 17th and 18th. And of course the Soviet press could hardly ignore the Premier's extensive travels abroad during the remainder of 1964, to Egypt, Hungary, and the Scandinavian countries.

3. *Pravda* and *Izvestia*, Dec. 13, 1962.

4. *Pravda*, Jul. 3; *Izvestia*, Jul. 4, 1963.

5. Dept. of State *Bulletin*, vol. 49, p. 239. *N.Y. Times*, Jul. 28, 1963.

6. *Pravda*, Jul. 14, 1963.

7. Sorensen, pp. 740–42.

8. *N.Y. Times*, Apr. 1, 4, 1963.

9. *Pravda* and *Izvestia*, Oct. 27, 1963.

10. Dept. of State *Bulletin*, vol. 49, pp. 694–97.

11. Instead of the expected 250 million, the Soviet Government purchased only 140 million dollars' worth of U.S. wheat during 1964. Soviet statistics being what they are, however, officials in Moscow can scarcely have been sure, even in November 1963, of the full extent of the shortage.

12. *N.Y. Times*, Nov. 27, 1963.

13. Salinger, p. 335.

CHAPTER 9

1. General Smith's Prefatory Note, pp. 7–8, to *Notes for a Journal*, falsely attributed to Litvinov (New York: William Morrow & Co., 1955). Litvinov made similar remarks to a journalist, Mr. Richard Hottelet, in June 1946. A serial account of this interview appeared in the *Washington Post*, January 21–25, 1952, a few days after Litvinov's death.

2. U.S., Dept. of State, *Foreign Relations of the United States, 1939* (Washington, D.C.: G.P.O., continuing series), I, 301–4.

3. Khrushchev's "secret'" speech to the Twentieth Party Congress in February 1956.

4. Peter Kleist, *Zwischen Hitler und Stalin* (Bonn: Athenäum Verlag, 1950), pp. 94–96. Paul Schmidt, *Statist auf diplomatischer Bühne* (Bonn: Athenäum Verlag, 1954), pp. 462–64.

5. *Pravda* and *Izvestia,* Feb. 13, 1957; translation from *Current Digest of the Soviet Press,* vol. 9, no. 11.

6. *Washington Post,* Dec. 18, 1962.

7. *Foreign Relations of the United States, 1940,* III, 406–8.

Selected Bibliography

ABEL, ELIE. *The Missile Crisis*. Philadelphia and New York: J. B. Lippincott, 1966.

Current Digest of the Soviet Press.

HILSMAN, ROGER. *To Move a Nation*. Garden City, N.Y.: Doubleday, 1967.

HORELICK, ARNOLD, L., and RUSH, MYRON. *Strategic Power and Soviet Foreign Policy*. Chicago and London: University of Chicago Press, 1966.

HYLAND, WILLIAM, AND SHRYOCK, RICHARD WALLACE. *The Fall of Khrushchev*. New York: Funk and Wagnalls, 1968.

Izvestia.

KENNEDY, ROBERT F. *Thirteen Days*. New York: W. W. Norton, 1969.

LAZO, MARIO. *Dagger in the Heart: American Policy Failures in Cuba*. New York: Funk and Wagnalls, 1968.

Neues Deutschland.

New York Times.

PAGE, MARTIN. *The Day Khrushchev Fell*. New York: Hawthorn Books, 1965.

PAUL, WOLFGANG. *Kampf um Berlin*. Munich and Vienna: Albert Langen, Georg Müller Verlag, 1962.

Pravda.

SALINGER, PIERRE. *With Kennedy*. Garden City, N.Y.: Doubleday, 1966.

SCHLESINGER, ARTHUR M., JR. *A Thousand Days: John F. Kennedy in the White House*. Boston: Houghton Mifflin, 1965.

SMITH, JEAN EDWARD. *The Defense of Berlin*. Baltimore: The Johns Hopkins Press, 1963.

SORENSEN, THEODORE C. *Kennedy*. New York: Harper and Row, 1965.

SPEIER, HANS. *Divided Berlin: The Anatomy of Soviet Political Blackmail.* New York: F. A. Praeger, 1961.

TATU, MICHEL. *Power in the Kremlin: From Khrushchev to Kosygin.* New York: Viking Press, 1969.

U.S. Department of State. *Bulletin.*

Washington Post.

WINDSOR, PHILIP. *City on Leave: A History of Berlin, 1945–1962.* New York: F. A. Praeger, 1963.

Index

Abel, Col. Rudolf, 95
Acheson, Dean, 128
Adenauer, Konrad, 54, 59, 77, 85, 173–74
Albania, 82, 160, 161, 162
Alsop, Joseph, 218–19
Anderson, Maj. Rudolf, Jr., 138
"Anti-Party group," 17, 158
Aragones Navarro, Emilio, 118
Austria, 19, 103, 193, 197
Autobahn: civilian traffic on, 55–56, 58, 59, 61, 95, 114, 152, 177, 179; military-police patrols on, 88, 94; arrests on, 88, 108–9, 177; military traffic on, 95, 100, 110, 114, 152 177, 180–81, 184–85, 187

Baku (Soviet vessel), 175
Baldwin, Hanson, 39, 40
Ball, George W., 115
Barghoorn, Prof. Frederick C., 185–86, 187
Beria, Lavrenti P., 12, 158, 219
Berlin, East: Westerners in, 56–57, 58, 61, 88–89, 94; Soviet commandant in, 69, 110; U.S. military in, 87, 94
Berlin, West: Khrushchev initiates "crisis" of, 43–44; barge traffic to, 56; 1948–49 blockade of, 57, 102, 195; U.S. garrison in, 86, 179; rail traffic to, 95; air traffic to, 95–100 *passim*, 108–9, 114, 176–77; Soviet "sour grapes" attitude toward, 99; importance of, 102; and Cuba, 105–10, 113–19 *passim*, 151–56; demonstrations in, 110–11; Soviet armor in, 112; Communist-front organization in, 154; residents al-

lowed to visit E. Berlin, 189. *See also* autobahn, Friedrichstrasse crossing, and Wall
Bizri, Gen. Afif, 20
Bohlen, Charles E., 50
Bolshakov, Georgi N., 83, 221
Brandenburg Gate, 89, 92, 112
Brandt, Willy, 59, 61, 85, 116, 117
Brezhnev, Leonid I., 64
Brodsky, Iosif, 223
Bulganin, Nikolai A., 21, 24
Bullitt, William, 193
Bundesrat, 71
Bundestag, 54, 71
Bundy, McGeorge, 83, 117, 127, 128

Capehart, Sen. Homer E., 117
Castro, Fidel: 148, 149; purges Communist, 104; announces fishing treaty, 122; demands of during missile crisis, 147; vetoes U.N. inspection, 148–49; and reconnaissance flights, 150; gives up IL-28's, 150–51.
Castro, Raul, 104–5
Catherine II, 11
Chen Yi, 31
Chiang Kai-shek, 30, 42
China, Communist: Soviet arms to, 35; conflict with U.S.S.R., 51, 158–64, 167–73, 178–79
Chou En-lai, 31, 34, 37–38, 82, 160
Clarke, Gen. Bruce C., 100
Clay, Gen. Lucius D., 86–87, 92, 100
Congress of Soviet Communist Party: 20th, 5, 159; 22nd, 5, 81, 160
Constitution, 11, 191
Cuba: Bay of Pigs landing in, 65; importance of, 103; Khrushchev's de-

cision on, 104–5; Soviet arms to, 105, 117–21 *passim;* surface to air missiles in, 118, 119, 125, 126; Soviet troops in, 119–20; Soviet naval base in, 122–23, 124; U.S. measures to reduce shipments to, 123; reconnaissance over, 125–26, 129, 135, 138, 143, 145–51 *passim,* 175; surface to surface missiles in, 126–27, 128, 134, 136, 138, 142–49 *passim,* 221, 222; and U.S. military measures, 128–29; blockade of, 128, 130, 131, 132, 135, 144, 147, 148, 151; IL-28 bombers in, 149, 150–51, 221; raids against, 175–76
Czechoslovakia, 46, 102, 103, 194

Daladier, Édouard, 193
Dillon, Douglas, 128
Dirksen, Sen. Everett M., 120
Dobrynin, Anatoly F.: 174, 180, 185, 188; warned by J. F. Kennedy re Berlin, 107–8; informed of Kennedy's Cuba speech, 130; warned by R. F. Kennedy re missiles, 143; reassuring statements to R. F. Kennedy and others, 221
Dodd, Sen. Thomas J., 181, 185
Dowling, Walter C., 57
Dulles, John Foster, 36–37, 42, **79,** 197

East Germany: U.S. aircraft in, 28–29, 52; Soviet peace treaty with, 52, 54, 70, 72, 75, 80–81, 98, 106–7, 108, 113, 153, 154–55; economic sanctions against, 58, 59–60, 85; escapees from, 75–76, 153; troops demobilized, **101, Party** program of, 154
Eisenhower, Dwight D.: 32, 36, 38, 41, 48, 66, 133; on Security Council summit, 29, 30; talks with Khrushchev, 45
Essoyan, Roy, 33, 39, 218–19

Fanfani, Amintore, 75
Fechter, Peter, 111

Ferrey, Gilbert, 95
"Fidel's Five Points," 147, 148, 150
Fields, 1st Lt. Raymond C., 180
Fischer, Louis, 17
Fomin, Alexander S., 135–36, 137, 140, 142, 143
Frankel, Max, 172
Freeman, Orville L., 174
Friedrichstrasse crossing: U.S. tanks at, 87, 89; tank confrontation at, 91, 92; Soviet tanks at, 93; U.S. retreat at, 93, 140, 160; Soviet bus attacked at, 111
Frost, Robert, 104
Fulbright, James William, 67

Gaitskell, Hugh, 21
Gaulle, Charles de, 29, 32, 64
Gavin, James M., 67
Gilpatric, Roswell L., 73, 149, 182
"Great Leap Forward," 51, 159, 160
Greece, 176
Greene, Hughie, **177**
Gromyko, Andrei A.: 81, 83, 98, 99, 101, 115, 153, 180, 187; and Syrian "crisis," 20–25 *passim;* talks with Thompson, 97; talks with Rusk, 108, 117; on Soviet naval base in Cuba, 122; reassuring remarks to Kennedy re Cuba, 124; and test-ban talks, 166
Grotewohl, Otto, 54
Guevara, Ernesto, 118

Hailsham, Quintin M. Hogg, Viscount, 166
Halleck, Rep. Charles A., 120
Hammarskjold, Dag, 30
Harriman, W. Averell, 166
Herter, Christian A., 55
Hilsman, Roger, 117, 125, 136
Hitler, Adolf, 13, 191, 193, 195–96
Home, Alexander Frederick Douglas-Home, Earl of, 98, 115, 167
Hottelet, Richard, 224
Humphrey, Sen. Hubert H., 174
Hungary: revolt in, 16, 19, 23, 46, 103
Hussein, King of Jordan, 20, 28, 41, 43

84; asked about Johnson, 188
Sandkrug Bridge, 112
Satellites, Soviet, 219
Scali, John, 135–37, 140, 142
Scheyven, Raymond, 114
Schröder, Gerhard, 179
Segni, Antonio, 75
Sixth Fleet, 20
Shaposhnikov, Marshal Boris M., 195
Shepilov, Dimitri T., 157, 197
Smirnov, Andrei A., 76, 77, 107, 110
Smith, Gen. Walter Bedell, 190
Solovyev, Col. (later Gen.) Andrei
   I., 88, 89, 101, 110
Sorensen, Theodore C., 84, 128, 221
Souvanna Phouma, Prince, 67
Spaak, Paul-Henri, 81
Stalin, Iosif V.: 12, 42, 158, 160, 170,
   173, 192; death of, 5; method of
   rule, 12, 219; on U.S. public opin-
   ion, 53; and Berlin blockade, 57,
   102; body removed from Red
   Square, 82; Khrushchev's use of,
   157; adulation of, 158; foreign
   policy of, 191; overconfidence of,
   194–95; dread inspired by, 195
State Department: organization of, 63
Steinhardt, Laurence A., 198
Stevenson, Adlai E., 136, 144–45,
   151, 166
Stoph, Willi, 109, 110
Suez crisis, 23, 27
Sulzberger, C. L., 80, 83, 84
Summit conferences: sought by
   Khrushchev, 27, 29–31, 97, 135;
   in Paris, 45–46, 49, 51–52; in Vi-
   enna, 68, 69, 70
Sylvester, Arthur, 145
Syria, 20

Tatan Island, 36
Taylor, Gen. Maxwell D., 127, 128
Test-ban treaty, 164–67, 171, 182
Tests, nuclear: resumed by U.S.S.R.,
   78, 82; canceled in Nevada, 165,
   177
Thompson, Llewellyn E., Jr.: 28, 68,
   84, 180; talks with Khrushchev,

29, 64; talks with Gromyko, 97;
   and wheat sales, 174
Tito, Josip, 194
Troops: U.S. withdrawal of from
   Europe, 179, 182–83
Truman, Harry S, 53, 196–97
Turkey: and Syrian "crisis," 20–23
   passim; U.S. missiles in, 138, 140,
   141, 143

Ulbricht, Walter: 54, 73; threats re
   W. Berlin, 60, 69; confers with
   Khrushchev, 98; flies to Russia,
   109; on peace-treaty deadline, 113;
   urges compromise, 154
U Thant, 135, 137, 148, 149, 150
U-2: shot down over China, 125; shot
   down over Cuba, 138, 222; flies
   over Chukchi Peninsula, 145
U-2 incident of 1960: 45, 64; Khrushchev's motives in, 46–48; public reaction to, 49; and reassuring statements by Khrushchev, 51; favorable results of, 53–54

Vansittart, Sir Robert, 63
Vietnam, 199–200

Wall, Berlin: 76, 77, 189; U.S. reaction to, 85; tank obstacles behind,
   92; shootings at, 111; Soviet troops
   patrolling, 153
Wang Chia-hsiang, 31
Watson, Gen. Albert E., 88, 89, 94
Wheat: Soviet purchases abroad, 173;
   U.S. sales of to U.S.S.R., 174–75,
   179, 181, 182, 184, 224

Yezhovshchina. See Purge, Soviet
Yugoslavia, 19, 27, 163, 171, 173

Zhukov, Georgi K.: 12, 14, 26; as
   rival of Khrushchev, 16; produces
   letter to Stalin, 17; popularity of,
   18; visit to Yugoslavia, 18, 21, 23–
   24; relieved as Defense Minister,
   23; expelled from Presidium and
   Central Committee, 25